MORE THEOLOGY &
LESS HEAVY CREAM

MORE THEOLOGY & *LESS HEAVY CREAM*

The Domestic Life *of* Pietro *and* Madeleine

by

ROBERT FARRAR CAPON

A MOCKINGBIRD
PUBLICATION

ISBN-13: 978-0-9907927-6-5
ISBN-10: 0-9907927-6-5

Mockingbird Ministries ("Mockingbird") is an independent
not-for-profit ministry seeking to connect, comment upon and
explore the Christian faith with and through contemporary
culture. Mockingbird disclaims any affiliation, sponsorship or
connection with any other entity using the words "Mockingbird"
and "Ministries" alone or in combination.

CONTENTS

The two characters you meet in More Theology and Less Heavy Cream *came to life early in my marriage to Robert. I made the morning coffee. Robert's response was, "Good coffee, Madeleine." Robert's alter ego, Pietro, began the conversations with Madeleine that appeared in these articles about food and theology. We had fun talking for many years about our two favorite subjects. Hope you enter into the joy as well.*

Valerie Capon
Shelter Island, NY 2016

PREFACE

by David Zahl

Midway through his book on the parables, Robert Capon takes an interlude to discuss the nature of hands. Not 'hired hands,' or hands as part of the Body of Christ, but hands as a metaphor for life. To get there, he draws out the contrast between a live hand and a dead one. A live hand, Robert says, takes the good things placed into it and clutches onto them, thereby closing itself off to other goods and gifts. A dead hand, meanwhile, simply lays there, open to whatever comes its way. A dead hand approximates the posture of Jesus, who did not consider life as "something to be grasped at."[1]

I like to think it would make Father Capon smile to know that dead-handedness played such a decisive role in reviving a few of his books that had fallen out of circulation, not to mention the one you are, er, clutching right now—which is seeing the light of day for the first time.

---

1. From *Kingdom, Grace, Judgment: Paradox, Outrage, and Vindication in the Parables of Jesus*, 256.

I should probably back up. Here's how this came to be: Our staff was running around one afternoon in early 2016, hustling to meet some deadline or other, when the phone rang. The voice on the line identified itself as the Rev. Mark Strobel, calling from Fargo, ND. He was familiar with our work and wanted to run something by us. Mark had recently been in touch with his good friend Valerie Capon, Robert's widow, and was curious to see if we had any interest in bringing some of her late husband's work back into print.

Come again?!

You see, Robert Farrar Capon has been one of Mockingbird's guiding lights since our founding in 2007. We were fortunate enough to publish the final interview he gave before his death in 2013. More than that, his name has become so ubiquitous in our work as to be embarrassing. It seems we can't host a conference, publish a book, or preach a sermon without referencing (or ripping him off) in some way. I was almost afraid to be in touch with his estate for fear that we would owe royalties.

An Episcopal clergyman, *New York Times* food critic, and author of twenty books that split the difference between those dual areas of interest, Robert was a rare breed. Advocates for the unflinching grace of God are hard enough to come by, in the church or elsewhere; to find one who can write—I mean, *really* write—that's another thing altogether. Some would say miraculous.

Reading Capon is a joyful and jolting experience, the opposite of boring. Words and turns of phrase leap off the page in Spirit-filled exuberance. Pastoral insight combines with rhetorical brilliance and uncontrived playfulness, not to mention the occasional snark, to produce something inspiring and maddening and utterly singular.

Unlike nearly all of his contemporaries, ecclesial or culinary, his reputation has only grown since he stopped writing—and in a surprisingly diverse number of circles. Evangelicals can't get enough of the unabashed Christocentrism. Progressives dig his radically non-moralistic approach to faith. Catholics can smell the reverence for the elements implicit in his appreciation for good wine and delicious bread. Foodies love the vivid prose and obvious delight in all things kitchen-related. Everyone enjoys the humor. It doesn't hurt that Twitter-friendly soundbites simply poured out of his pen.

But Fr. Capon was also that rare scholar whose love of the Bible was truly contagious, a provocateur after God's own heart, unafraid to follow the Good News into every crevice of human experience, emphasis on *good*. The man didn't just talk about freedom, it dripped from his every sentence. Among the stacks of memorable encapsulations of the Christian message he left us, one favorite would have to be:

> If there is a God who can take the dead and, without a single condition of credit-worthiness or a single, pointless promise of reform, raise them up whole and forgiven, free for nothing—well, that would not only be wild and wonderful; it would be the single piece

of Good News in a world drowning in an
ocean of blame.[2]

Intimidated as I was by Rev. Strobel's invitation, I could
not deny that there was something strangely, well, *Capon-
esque* about the manner in which it arrived, i.e., dropped
into an open, undeserving palm. Furthermore, in pretty
much everything he wrote, Robert had identified himself
not just with the foolishness of the Cross but with fools
themselves. So maybe the association was fitting after
all. It was certainly the only grounds on which we could
deign to accept such a project. I mean, what did we have
to lose? If Robert was right, the (divine) accountants have
all been laid off, the religion shop closed, the scorekeep-
ing union disbanded for good. We might as well give it
a shot.

So here we are, still pinching ourselves that this is
happening, laughing at God's sense of humor, and hope-
ful that you will find yourself laughing along with us soon.
Most of all, we look forward to the day when we get to
bask in the ridiculousness of it all with Robert himself.
I can picture the banquet now, thanks in no small part
to the man himself. There'll be cigars and brandy and an
ungodly amount of butter. It'll be extravagant, none too
dignified, and overcrowded. Fortunately, he won't be hard
to find—the life of the party never is.

A quick note about this book. *More Theology & Less*

---

2. From his indispensible preface to *The Romance of the Word* in 1994,
probably the best starting point for those interested in delving deeper.

Heavy Cream is the sequel to a collection of Robert's work called *Light Theology & Heavy Cream: The Culinary Adventures of Pietro & Madeleine,* published by Cowley Publications in 2004. That volume introduced readers unfamiliar with *The Wittenburg Door* (the sadly defunct—and intentionally misspelled—humor/theology magazine where much of the content originally appeared) to the Capons' memorable alter egos, lovable blowhard Pietro and his long-suffering better half Madeleine. Both this book and that one excerpt a number of the couple's dialogues over dinner prep. Some of their conversations are dead serious, many are not, most are a mixture. All of them are full of wit and wisdom and an abundance of lighthearted sparring.

The variety of topics reflects Robert's refreshing refusal to compartmentalize his passions. They range from the length of time needed to knead bread properly and virtues of "irenic belligerence" in times of war to the resurrection of the dead and the mission of the church in the world. You'll hear them sound off on the relationship between peppers and perspiration, the exasperating notion of "Christian music," and one of Robert's abiding themes, clerical infidelity.

Aside from adding a few footnotes and correcting a handful of typos, the manuscript stands exactly as Robert intended you to read it. Call me fanciful, but I like to think he conceived of it as a meal in its own right, each course carefully constructed to compliment the one that came before, some slight, others more substantial, a palette cleanser followed by an entree, adding up to a grace-infused whole.

If so, then all that remains for me to do is to invite you to raise your glass to Pietro, may he rest in peace, and repeat after me: *"Bon appetit! And amen."*

Charlottesville, Virginia
November 2016

INTRODUCTION

PIETRO & MADELEINE
REINTRODUCE THEIR CREATOR

As we did in our previous book, *Light Theology and Heavy Cream: The Culinary Adventures of Pietro and Madeleine*, we greet you as the creatures of our author's vivid if whimsical imagination. Once again, all the pieces in this book were composed by him between 1978 and 1988, with the indispensable help of his wife, Valerie. They were originally published in either *The Wittenburg Door* (which was then the *Mad Comics* of evangelical journalism)[3], or on the food pages of the Long Island daily, *Newsday*. As before, he has made no effort to update references to persons, events, or controversies of those times. It has been said that those who will not remember the past are doomed to repeat it. Our literary creator feels that since so many of the ills he stigmatized in these pieces are still far too much with us, it is

---

3. *The Wittenburg Door* was a bimonthly satire magazine to which Capon regularly contributed.

1

best to leave the lessons of their follies as originally taught.

He also finds divine precedent for this policy. Jesus, we believe, is the Word of God who makes all things for his Father's glory to begin with, and who becomes incarnate in our flesh, to restore all things to end with. Accordingly, Jesus saves our past in two paradoxical but delicious flavors: exactly as it was in ourselves with all its tackiness and tawdriness, and exactly as it has always been in all its glory as he has held it from the foundation of the world. In short, he takes all our sins and follies into himself in his death on the cross, and he re-members them—he puts them all back together gloriously—in the reconciliation of his resurrection. Like the lost sheep, we may have been lost in ourselves, but from the start we have always been found in him.

Since that is the greatest joke ever told to a supremely unfunny world, we commend this second *smorgasbord* to you as enthusiastically as we did the first, and we congratulate Mockingbird on their bravery in letting us turn to the sheer fun of faith. We feel that given the irony of a God who saves the world by foolishness and weakness, and the hilarity by which he gives us corn, wine, and oil—not to mention such two-faced creatures as butter, salt, tobacco, and pork fat—this is no world in which to land on one side of a paradox. Once again then, nibble away.

You have nothing to lose but your straight face and your narrow waistline,

Pietro and Madeleine
Shelter Island, NY

ONE

THEOLOGY AND WHITE WINE

"We've been cloned!" Madeleine exclaimed, putting down the copy of *The Wittenburg Door* Pietro had handed her to read. "Doesn't that make you feel creepy?"

"Actually," Pietro said calmly, "I rather like Renaldo and Margaret—especially Margaret. She seems to have her head just a tad more tightly threaded on than he."[4]

"He had some valid points, if you ask me," Madeleine said. "You do get a bit one-sided, you know, with all that radical faith-and-grace talk."

Pietro yawned. "All that radical faith-and-grace talk

---

4. In his usual fashion, Capon intended this book to start with a bang—Chapter One finds itself in the middle of a *Wittenburg Door* feud, which began with its 86th issue (Feb-March 1986), in which Capon wrote a "Pietro and Madeleine" column about the distinction between faith and theology. To express his disagreement, a reader named Kevin Gowen submitted a mock-column featuring "Renaldo and Margaret" entitled, "In Defence of Theology." This chapter is Capon's response to Gowen's response. As *The Door* editors wrote, "This ought to be fun."

was once, in happier times, referred to as the very nub of the Reformation insight and the heart of the Gospel. Nevertheless, Renaldo's theological exuberances are well-written and therefore forgivable. I am reminded of Auden on Yeats:

'Time that with this strange excuse
Pardoned Kipling and his views,
And will pardon Paul Claudel,
Pardons him for writing well.'"

"Not so fast into the sleep of reason," Madeleine threatened. "I want to hear you answer some of his points, not just write him off as pardonable."

Pietro resigned himself to a later bedtime and refilled his pipe. He lit up, then did an imaginary accordion shuffle with his hands. "Pick a point, my little chickadee," he said; "pick any point you like. Look! Nothing up my sleeves."

She ignored the W.C. Fields act and pressed him on the first point. "Okay," she said, "Renaldo says theology provides faith with content and direction. What do you say?"

"Don't like it," Pietro replied peremptorily. "Evangelicals—at least a fair number of evangelicals—have recently discovered two wonderful new stimulants, namely, theology and white wine; and they have gone slightly gah-gah over both of them. True enough, both thinking and drinking are delightful projects with which to grace an afternoon or enliven an evening; but as one who has kept a wine cellar since 1953 and a theology attic since well before that, I assure you that neither of those repositories of my hopes ever quite delivered what I expected of them in my first enthusiasms. Theology does not provide faith with content. The content of faith is Jesus as displayed in the Gospel narratives in particular and in the Scriptures generally. All theology does is receive that content and juggle it around as best it can. And if Renaldo reminds me that the Bible is already loaded with theology about Jesus—that is, with theological content in addition to just plain Jesus—I will tell him I know that. But I also know that its theological content is of many different sorts: Matthean, Lucan, Pauline, Petrine, Johannine. It's not just one, grand, correct, final synthesis called Orthodox Christian Theology."

"Maybe we should go to bed," Madeleine observed, regretting her insistence on an answer.

Pietro counter-ignored the implied accusation of heaviness. "And as for theology providing faith with direction…well, I have an uneasy feeling about that. It would seem to me that if you feel the need to postulate some direction for faith, you simply say 'toward Jesus' and let it go at that. But I'm afraid Renaldo has a rather more complicated bee in his bonnet when he talks about direction. He's worried about how to convince people they ought to point themselves toward Jesus rather than (to use his example) James Jones, the instigator of the mass suicide at the Jamestown community. He's concerned, in short, not with faith but with the question of how to decide between rival candidates for faith."

"So?" Madeleine said curtly. "What's wrong with that?"

"Nothing," Pietro said amiably, "as long as he realizes that what he's actually talking about is *apologetics*, not just theology pure and simple. His real agenda is convincing people, by sound theological arguments, that evangelical Christians are not just a bunch of blind-faith anti-rationalists who have been blown into a permanent tizzy by biblical criticism and scientific knowledge."

"So?" Madeleine said twice as curtly. "What's wrong with *that*?"

"Nothing," Pietro said twice as amiably, "as long as he's aware that he's using theology to win a popularity contest, not to do its proper work. We are called to be fools for Christ's sake and to proclaim the foolishness by which God saves the world. But Renaldo's professed desire is for us to be wise—to show the world, as he says, that we are not drooling idiots—to be able to prove that we can stand right up there at the bar of contemporary thought and knock back shot for shot with the disputers of this world."

Madeleine started to say "So?" again, but Pietro cut her off.

"I think two of those exchanges are sufficient for one evening," he said. "Permit me to continue. My objection to apologetics—or better said, to the exaltation of apologetics as the prime work of theology—is that it is a far less convincing enterprise than anyone thinks. Those who live in the hope—or worse yet, in the assurance—that they have some invincibly true theological arguments which will enable the world to distinguish, infallibly and universally, between Jesus and Jones are probably in for a disappointment."

"You leave no room for apologetics at all, then?"

"Of course I leave room," Pietro replied. "I just happen to think that theological argument is not the best apologetic. If I come up to you and say, 'I can prove that lobsters exist!'—and you've never even heard of lobsters—all you're going to do is yawn. But if I come up to you with fabulous and fascinating stories about lobsters—about their physiology, their habits, their culinary uses, their gustatory possibilities—then, *after you're thoroughly fascinated*, it might be time to entertain you with a proof that there are such things as lobsters. The best apologetic, therefore, is what it always was: the old, weird, incomprehensible, great, gray-green, greasy Gospel story—just laying out in front of people the Jesus of Scripture who alone can knock the world's socks off."

"But what about Renaldo's claim that *bad* theology actually prevents people from hearing what Jesus says? Don't you need *good* theology to drive out bad?"

Pietro smiled broadly. "Of course you do. I am entirely *with* Renaldo on the negative function of theology—and with his insistence that, since everybody theologizes, there is a definite need for Christians to do it particularly well. He and I, after all, are both devotees of the gentleman who wrote *The Romance of the Word: One Man's Love Affair With Theology*."

TWO

INVASION OF THE CREAM SNATCHERS

"What went wrong last night?" Madeleine asked in disbelief. "You've made that heavy cream sauce a thousand times. How come, at the one dinner party I rave about it in advance, you make it too thin?"

Pietro looked downcast. "I just can't cook when people like Irving watch me. You should have kept him in the dining room where he couldn't shame me into not using enough butter and cream."

"You? Ashamed? About using butter and cream? I've been trying to inhibit you for years. You mean all I have to do to lose weight is stand in the kitchen and look over your shoulder?"

"No," Pietro said. "With you it wouldn't work. You're different."

"Different? How?" she asked. "Other than that I'm a prisoner in Fat City?"

"No, no. That's a compliment. A person can cook

9

around you without feeling guilty. If he starts to salt something, you don't lay a low-sodium trip on him. If he wants to add butter, you don't scream *'Calories!'* If he puts in more cream, you actually smile."

"Stop, already. Your idea of a compliment sounds like my idea of a confession."

"All I mean to say is that you judge food on the basis of whether it tastes good, so it's a pleasure to cook for you," Pietro said as his eyes brightened a bit.

"Well! Thank you, I think. But what other basis is there?" Madeleine queried.

Pietro sighed. "Unfortunately, there is the basis most other people use—the one that makes them, like Irving, a pain in the kitchen. They pay attention, not to food, but to fads."

"How so?"

"Think of cream, for instance. To you it's just a delectable substance to be spooned, ladled, poured or slathered in all directions. In your perfectly reasonable view, an entire container of it—plus, of course, some onion, a splash of white wine, a bit of reduced stock and a judicious pinch of salt—would make barely enough sauce for two sautéed chicken breasts. Is that correct?"

"Unfortunately."

"No, fortunately. You should be thankful to be so far from the fadding crowd—from ignoble Irving and all the rest of the nutritional nudges. Do you know what cream is to them?"

"What?"

"It's not cream at all. Instead, it's whatever the journalistico-medico-dietetic establishment has frightened them into calling it this year."

"You mean, like, calories?"

"That was last year's scare, but it will do for an illustration. A *calorie* is a measurement, not a thing. It is no more a real being than an *inch* is. Therefore to judge food on the basis of calories—to look at a cup of cream and have as one's principal reaction the words '800 calories'— is as irrelevant as looking at a copy of the Declaration of Independence and saying '32 inches'. Or, come to think of it, '800 calories': a large copy might well give off just that much heat."

"Aha! So Irving gave you a lecture on calories, huh?" Madeleine asked elatedly.

"No. That would never have fazed me. He did something worse," Pietro answered gloomily.

"What? He accused you of pumping your guests full of cholesterol?"

"Hardly. I would have been ready for that one, too. Cream contains dozens of chemicals, some of which may not sit well with certain unfortunate creatures. But at the level to which those substances are present in even a generous dose of cream, they have yet to be proved harmful to ordinary, healthy people. No. If Irving had badgered me with such nonsense, I would have laughed in his face. I'm afraid he was cleverer than that."

"You make him sound demonic. What on earth did he do?" Madeleine questioned impatiently.

"He didn't *do* anything. He just stood there and *thought*. I could feel the brain waves."

"You actually felt him *thinking*? About what, for heaven's sake?"

"Calories. Sodium. Cholesterol. Obesity. High blood pressure. Arterial plaque. All of it."

"But you have an answer for every one of those things."

"True. But not to all of them at once, just hanging, unspoken in the air. It was as if there was a dietetic grease fire in his head and the kitchen was full of intellectual smoke. My mind couldn't breathe."

"You're saying, then, that Irving jammed your thoughts? That's why you forgot to add enough cream?"

Pietro hung his head. "I wish it were that simple. Actually, I remembered, but I lost my nerve."

"What? You mean he thought so hard about nutrition that he broke your will or something? I can't believe that," Madeleine exclaimed, as she shook her head in utter disbelief.

"No. He thought another thought. They always do, you know."

"You make it sound terrible. What did he think?"

"He used their ultimate weapon. He said to himself: *'Pietro is not a good person'*. My convictions collapsed on the spot."

"That's ridiculous. You're the stubbornest cook in the world," Madeleine stated almost proudly.

"He got me to hold back on the cream, didn't he?"

"Hmmm," she said.

"But you don't think I'm a bad person, do you?"

"Hmmm," she said again.

"Please," Pietro begged. "Tell me I'm not."

"Hmmm," Madeleine mused the third time. "Maybe I can go on that diet after all."

THREE

BED AND BOARD

Pietro was making Danish pastry on his day off. Even if he said so himself, he had terrific moves. Rolling up the cinnamon-scented, raisin-studded sheet of dough, he sealed the edge smartly with tap water, sliced the roll into uniform schnecken with rapid-fire strokes of the knife and had them panned and rising in nothing flat.

He turned to the companion of his bed and board. "There," he said triumphantly. "It'll be gorgeous. Guaranteed." Madeleine was cutting up celery for tunafish salad—as usual, she was preoccupied.

Why, he wondered, did she have to work so slowly? When she peeled potatoes, she sat down at the table and laboriously deposited each paring into the center of a paper towel. When he did vegetables, he stood at the sink, flipped the peels all over the place and got the job done in one third the time. He would lighten her darkness.

"Hey, love, why are you dicing that celery one stalk

15

at a time? And with that dinky knife? If you used my chef's knife and cut them all lengthwise first, you could cut them crosswise all at once. Efficiency, kid. That's the name of the game."

Madeleine threw the paring knife down on the board. "Look. If I wanted somebody to do time and motion studies on me, I'd have taken up with a choreographer, not a pastry-pushing advice-peddler. At least he'd be interested in my moves someplace besides the kitchen. And don't call me 'kid'. I'm old enough to dice celery anyway I like. Why don't you grow up and learn that when you're not doing something you shouldn't bother people who are? Finish the salad yourself!"

Pietro followed her down the hallway only to have the bedroom door slammed in his face. By the time he fetched a wooden skewer to pop the lock, she was sobbing into her second tear-soaked pillow. "Look, Maddie, all I meant was…" That tore it.

Somebody once defined an expert as an ordinary man a long way from home. Nobody, Pietro thought to himself as she lit into him with a week's worth of grievances, was much of a marriage counselor in his own bedroom. Still, there was nothing for it now but to take the full treatment. Ten minutes of tirade were followed by seven of silence and thirty-five of dredging the channels of communication. At the end, he formulated—*to* her but *for* himself—yet another of Pietro's Pet Principles: *If You're Not Doing It, Don't.* He swore on the stack of rumpled bedclothes that he would keep his nose out of her celery-dicing forever.

The bedclothes became still more rumpled after that and, twenty minutes later, while she freshened up, a renewed man returned to the kitchen to tackle the tunafish. All went well until it came time for the mayonnaise. The jar was empty. For an instant, he was tempted to shout the bad news down the hall.

It occurred to him just in time, that there was a corollary to his recently hatched Principle which was just as important: *If You Are Doing It, Do It All.* He got out an egg, a lemon, salt, and olive oil, and whipped up a batch of homemade mayonnaise in the blender right on the spot. Tasting it, he was moved to take back some of the cynical things he had depressed himself with recently.

He had worked all week long with an unlikeable couple whose contempt for each other was as deserved as it was implacable. He had given them extra hours for nothing. The counseling had helped, but it had also backfired: They had come divided by mutual hatred; they left united in anger at him. At a cocktail party last night he learned they were bad-mouthing him all over town. No good deed, Pietro reflected bitterly, goes unpunished.

But now—Pollyanna be praised—his virtuous resolve not to shout a complaint had paid off in honest-to-God mayonnaise, the first in months. Virtue was indeed, its own reward.

Pietro put the finished salad into a container and turned to the task of transferring the rest of the mayonnaise from the blender to a jar. The job had always annoyed him—all those air pockets getting trapped in the jar, necessitating patient and repeated pounding on the counter till they rose to the surface. *Gentle* pounding, though, on a potholder or a thick towel. He had more than once ended up with a counterful of mayonnaise and broken glass.

Was there a lesson here, too? Pietro felt for a moment that his starchier colleagues might take a dim view of the culinary approaches to counseling that were coming so thick and fast this morning. But intellectual respectability be damned: Anything can be an illustration, just as long as it sheds light.

This bout he had just had with Madeleine: What was that, if it wasn't the settling of the mayonnaise of their marriage to get rid of the pockets of silence and the air-holes of distance they had accumulated during seven days of not dealing with each other? Their exertion in the bedroom worked in the same way as this lesser operation in the kitchen. And it operated under the same necessities: It had to be done; it could not be done halfheartedly; and it was dangerous if not done gently.

But it resulted in a product with a longer shelf life. Let his colleagues call that corn if they liked. It wasn't bad for a day off.

He checked his Danish. The schnecken were coming along nicely, but another half-hour or so wouldn't hurt. Was there a lesson somewhere that could be drawn from dough? Warmth as the key to rising? He noted that Madeleine had not yet emerged from the bedroom. Perhaps he might wander down the hall again and work out a corollary or two with her.

Pietro whistled as he went.

FOUR

UP WITH DOWN

"Well!" said Madeleine, sorting through the mail. "Here's one for the books. *The Wittenburg Door* has tripped over its own land mine. They're going to take up that ridiculous dare and produce a completely straight issue."[5]

Pietro continued to pass through the room. "I am practicing mellow today," he said grandly; "it will take more than that to disturb the *wah* of my house. *The Door* is as entitled to make mistakes as anyone. If they want to sell their birthright for a mess of promotional pottage, that is their business. I shall simply pray that they repent early and often of this dereliction from their calling."

Madeleine had little respect for mellow and no sympathy at all for its practitioners. "We'll see about that," she said, pulling an aggravating rabbit out of the hat. "This postcard says you have a deadline of a week from now to

---

5. "The Nice Issue," November 1986. Pietro, as Robert's alter-ego, was also a columnist for *The Door*.

write them something positive rather than negative."

Pietro wheeled furiously in the hallway and was suddenly all alarms and excursions. "Let me see that," he said, rushing back into the room. "I can't believe this. They actually expect me to participate in such folly? Never! To be negative is not a vice; it is simply the necessary complement of being positive. Only the loosest sort of intellectually trendy lips prattle on against negativity."

"Well, then," Madeleine said airily, "just tell them you won't write it."

"Oh…well, now," Pietro said, struggling to recover his misplaced mellow; "I don't know about *that*. No…of course I shall write it. It's just that I cannot truckle to philosophical hashmakers. You must help me, though; I need a calming rather than provoking atmosphere."

"Why don't I give you some ideas, then?" Madeleine said brightly.

"You mean, you've got the whole piece figured out already?" he asked, daring to hope for light at the end of this tunnel.

"No silly," she said. "All I mean is that I could sort of freely associate, and you could flesh the whole thing out with words."

Pietro bit his tongue. The light at the end of the tunnel had turned out to be Jersey, but there was nothing for it but to press on. "Very well then," he said, cranking up his best Academy Awards style: "For the freest association on the subject of the philosophical differences between positivity and negativity…may I have the envelope, please?"

"Batteries," Madeleine said.

"Batteries? That's all?"

"Why not? They've got positive and negative."

"Hmm," Pietro mused. "Batteries. If you hook two positive terminals together, you get nothing. Ditto, two negatives. But with one of each you get a flow of electricity. Aha! *The Door* is supposed to be giving the church a jolt of the old Gospel juice. But if it accentuates only the positive and eliminates the negative, it'll just end up as one more dead, dry cell." Pietro paused, scribbled a note and looked up. "Okay, next envelope, please."

"Sauces," Madeleine said.

"What about sauces?"

"What you always say about them: lemon, salt...you know."

Pietro got the drift. "Oh, right," he said. *The Door* as the church's *chef saucier*—the one who knows how to wake up tired ecclesiastical gravy with the salt of satire and the lemon juice of lampoon. *The Door*, therefore must not listen to anti-sodium moralists who want no salty fare, nor to bland theologizers who will not allow the acid of wit..."

"Fine, fine," Madeleine broke in. "You ready for another envelope?"

"Oh," Pietro said, quickly jotting down key words. "Yes, indeed. And thank you, by the way. You are nothing less than the Price, Waterhouse of my life."

Madeleine ignored this. "Next association: a blind man walking toward the edge of a cliff."

Pietro was getting the hang of it now. "Ah, easy," he crowed. "*The Door* as the only voice that refuses to talk as if the church knows where it's going. The only voice that does not comfort it, reason with it, or plead with it, but instead simply shouts—to the accompaniment of hand buzzers and whoopee cushions—'STOP!' in a voice loud enough to keep it from going straight over the cliffs of its own idiocy."

Madeleine was ready with another, but Pietro cut her off. "Wait, wait," he said. "There are more nominations in the blind man category. There's the donkey and the two-by-four: *The Door* as the only magazine willing to do *anything* to get the church's attention—up to and including whacking it on the head with the often tasteless and admittedly sophomoric Green Weenie Award. And for another, the little boy in the crowd: *The Door* as the church's Kiddy Komics—the one periodical so innocent of what a serious Christian publication ought to be like that it actually manages now and then to spot a king with no clothes on."

Madeleine finally broke in: "Are you ready for the last one, or not?" she asked impatiently.

Pietro bowed graciously and put out his hand. "May I have the final envelope, please?"

Leaning forward with a Cheshire cat grin only she could manage, Madeleine beamed, "The Wittenberg door."

Pietro looked perplexed, "*The Wittenburg Door*? Isn't that the *subject* of all these associations? How can it be one of the associations themselves?"

"It can be if you spell it right."

"Ah!" Pietro agreed. "Clever of you. You mean '-berg', as in Germany, rather than '-burg', as on the magazine's misspelled masthead. Very good: Luther's Ninety-Five Theses as something less than a totally positive approach to the Church's problems in the sixteenth century, and therefore *The Door* as justified in using not entirely un-negative methods in the Twentieth."

"And how about the actual word 'protestant'," Madeleine chimed in. "You can't get much more negative than that."

"I don't know," Pietro said. "Etymologically, it comes from 'testify for'. Some smart aleck would be sure to point that out."

"Etymology is piffle," Madeleine said. "Protestant is a wonderful, negative word, and you know it."

"Piffle, you say, eh?"

"Yes," she said. "And if *The Door* has any brains, it'll stop all this boring, positive talk and go right on saying 'piffle' till Kingdom come."

FIVE

RISING TO THE OCCASION

"What I fail to understand," Madeleine said edgily, "is why you invariably end up in these tête-à-têtes about breadmaking—and, I might add, why they always seem to be with the flashiest women at the party."

"The first question, I can answer," Pietro replied. "The second, I wouldn't touch with a barge pole."

"Aha! Then you admit it's the lookers who get the longest sessions."

"I admit nothing of the sort. As a matter of fact most of my time this evening was spent with your cousin's husband—a gentleman for whom 'unprepossessing' is the only word even Charity herself could find. Go back to question one."

"Very well. Why can't you just give your little disciples a complete recipe right from the start? After all, I presume it *is* cooking instruction you're giving, not marriage counseling."

"Many a true word is spoken in jest," Pietro parried. "You have just handed me the perfect analogy."

"How's that?"

"Because a complete recipe for making bread—that is, one that anticipated all of the 10,374 lions that lie in the way of the exercise—would be as useless as telling engaged couples that babies eventually turn into teenagers. The warning is so bizarre as to be unbelievable."

"You mean to say you couldn't mention even a few of the pitfalls? Ministers do it all the time in premarital instruction."

"That is because ministers know that between sex, romance and the fact that the invitations are already printed, it is practically impossible to daunt the novices of matrimony. Fledgling breadbakers have far fewer inducements to persistence. The tiny flame of their enthusiasm…"

"Oh, come now," Madeleine said. "Tiny flame indeed! Your friend Melissa, if I may mention a name, is about as quenchable as a brush fire in a high wind."

"Ah," Pietro observed blandly. "Once again you prove my point. Allow me to take Melissa, for example."

"No! *I'll* take her—for a long walk on a short pier."

"At least *my* response to her problem didn't involve the police. She was, it seems, unable to produce proper free-standing loaves. Her French bread always ended up with the cross-section of a bedroom slipper and the density of uranium."

"Serves her right."

"The poor girl was, in fact, about to spring for expensive flour and special baguette pans. But I spared her."

"Rats!"

"First, I advised her to use only ordinary bread flour—the commercial high-gluten stuff now packaged for domestic use and sold in supermarkets. It makes the most elastic dough."

"How come you didn't tell her that from the start?"

"Because at the start, most people bake bread in pans, where elasticity is not a supreme necessity. Why trouble them with instructions they don't need?"

"I don't know. Troubling Melissa just seemed like a good idea."

"I ignore that and pass on. Next, I asked her to tell me truthfully how long she kneaded her bread."

"And she lied, right?"

"No. To do her credit, she admitted she had never kept at it for the full fifteen minutes needed to develop the gluten. She'd been told about that from the start, of course, but disbelief led her to ignore it. Proof positive, you see, that even minimal instruction is sometimes too much."

"It's you who's too much."

"Be that as it may, since she was now aware, as she could never have been before, of the desirability of developing the gluten, I added the advice to give the dough two three-minute rests during the kneading—advice which, you must admit, would be even more incredible to a beginner."

"This whole subject is incredible."

Pietro shrugged. "Finally, having guaranteed that her bread would now rise to roundness instead of falling flat, I addressed myself to the problem of leaden texture. I asked her how long she let her shaped loaves rise before baking."

"And?"

"She said, 'An hour'. I told her that since the commonest fault in homemade bread is underproofing, she should give them two hours in a moist atmosphere at 85°—a direction which, to a mind unfocused by failure, would sound like nothing but the most flagrant high churchiness."

"And that was it?"

"Not quite. She wanted to know how to get loaves with sesame seeds all over them. So, rather than risk confusing her with a lot of talk about rolling the shaped loaves in beaten eggwhite and then in sesame seeds and *then* letting them rise, I invited her to be one of the lucky ones to watch next time I bake."

"You didn't!"

"Oh. Sorry about that. What I meant to say was: Rather than risk *inviting* her, I confused her with a lot of talk about…"

"Now *you're* the lucky one."

SIX

QUICK STUDY

"What do you want me to do with this rice, Aunt Madeleine? Save it or throw it out?"

Madeleine's visiting niece held up a pot for her inspection. "There's a whole pile left. Why does Uncle Peter cook so much when there's only three of us?"

Her aunt shook her head as she stacked the dishwasher. "I don't know, Cynthia. I think when God made your uncle, he forgot to put an 'off' button on his rice switch. He always cooks too much and then just forgets about it. Still, maybe we better save it. Dump it in one of those clean ricotta containers and put it in the fridge."

Pietro appeared suddenly in the kitchen doorway. "One irreverence I might suffer patiently. Likewise an isolated falsehood or a single piece of gross impracticality. But when I hear all three tossed together in a veritable salad of errors, I have no choice but to rise from my wine and come to the defense of truth."

"What *are* you babbling about?" Madeleine asked. "Cynthia and I are simply trying to clean up the mess you left out here."

"You are not *simply* doing any such thing," Pietro retorted. "You are threatening to complicate this innocent child's whole future as a cook." He turned to the girl solicitously. "It isn't exactly that your Auntie Madeleine is a bad person, Cynthia; it's just that she sometimes doesn't see the larger picture. You must learn to take her with a grain of salt."

"Aunt Madeleine says when you talk like that I should take you with a whole box of it."

Pietro shook his head sadly. "Alas, 'Evil communications corrupt good manners'—if I may quote St. Paul's quote. Nevertheless, let me try to correct your aunt's errors. In years to come, you will thank me."

Cynthia looked over his shoulder to Madeleine.

Madeleine rolled her eyes at Cynthia.

Cynthia returned a rapt gaze to Pietro.

"Excellent," Pietro said, having missed the entire exchange. "An attentive child is a teacher's delight. Let us first deal with the practical error. If you want to be a truly efficient cook, Cynthia, you will never put cold rice away in containers. Those who do so run afoul of a phenomenon as inexorable as the law of gravity: It is one of the principles of the universe that, while the first container you select will invariably be too small—and so be just one more thing to wash up—the second container will by the same necessity always be too large, thus surrounding your rice with that archenemy of good food storage, air. To avoid both disasters, therefore, you put your leftovers in plastic bags."

Pietro demonstrated. "See? You shake the rice down in one corner and snugly twist the bag shut. It not only has no air, but it looks nice. Rather like a big, white candy-kiss, don't you think? Appearances count, Cynthia. Always remember that."

Pietro put the bag in the fridge.

Cynthia rolled her eyes at Madeleine.

"Now," Pietro said, "as to the falsehood. Your aunt has no right to say I forget about leftover rice. It just so happens that my way of remembering things is to wait for her to accuse me of having forgotten them. And, since she spouts such accusations as regularly as Old Faithful, there is in fact no chance of my really forgetting anything at all, is there?"

Cynthia puzzled for a moment, then nodded yes and said no at the same time.

Pietro took it as agreement and pressed on. "Finally, however, as to the deepest error of all. Hear me clearly, dear child: There is no such thing as too much rice. The more you put in the fridge, the more it miraculously causes other leftovers to disappear. Do you know how it does that, Cynthia?"

"My mother says baking soda eats smells. Maybe leftover rice eats other food."

"Not quite," Pietro said. "Actually, the rice makes *us* eat the other food. If there's leftover milk, for instance, and you open the refrigerator door, the rice screams at you, 'Make rice pudding!' Or, if there's celery, carrots, and peppers, it shouts, 'Make rice salad!' And if there's a little bacon, eggs, and lettuce, it says, '*Chow fun!*'—which is Chinese for fried rice. It even knows languages, you see. That's because, when God created leftover rice, he made it extra smart. He knew that some day Benjamin Franklin would invent the ice box and that, unless there was something more intelligent than people around to use it, there'd be an awful lot of wasted food."

"Oh, wow!" said Cynthia. "Lucky for Aunt Madeleine she saved the rice, huh?"

"Not just for her, Cynthia. The whole world is a better place when we understand these things."

SEVEN

CIVIL DISOBEDIENCE

"It just galls me," Madeleine said, "the way some preachers trot out Romans 13 every time anyone dares suggest that the government might not always be infallible, incorruptible, and impeccable. Can you believe that sermon we just heard? A couple of rinkydink churches provide sanctuary for a handful of ragtag political refugees, and he pulls out all the stops on the wickedness of civil disobedience—'the powers that be are ordained of God.' Pliggle!"

"Pliggle?" Pietro queried as they walked across the church parking lot. "I am unfamiliar with the word. Is it a technical term? A category of biblical criticism, perhaps?"

"No, it's a polite way of avoiding barnyard language. But it still expresses total disapproval."

"You have problems, then, with the Reverend Mr. Meddlemore's views on the relationship between church and state?"

Madeleine got to the car first and climbed into the

driver's seat. "I have problems with Ernest Meddlemore, period. He's got a brain that's limper than the Bible he flaps at his congregation. He actually thinks Ronald Reagan is the Lord's Anointed."

Pietro let himself in the other door and belted up. "Well, my dear," he said soothingly, "Mr. Meddlemore is just one more standee in church history's long line of Erastian clerics. Wish him repentance and a better mind and take me home for a glass of chardonnay. This noontime earnestness after Sunday services is hazardous to my soul's health."

Madeleine held the car keys over her purse and ostentatiously dropped them back in. "You get your wine only if you stop with the puns and give me a little honest feedback. What's Erastianism, anyway?"

"It's a catchbasket term for a bunch of reformation notions, all of which pretty much boil down to the idea that the state has the right to tell the church where to head in. Erastus himself probably wasn't much of an Erastian, but his name got hung on such propositions as the King of England being head of the church, Parliament having the power to revise the Book of Common Prayer, the civil magistrate in Geneva having the right of excommunication, and so on."

"What's all that got to do with Ernest Meddlemore and the Nicaraguan refugees?" Madeleine asked.

"You must pardon me my dear," Pietro said, "but to my freely associating ear, 'Ernest Meddlemore and the Nicaraguan Refugees' sounds like either the title of a Tom

Swift book or the name of a rock group."

Madeleine made fists and shook them in front of her face. "I will *not* pardon you! Stop with the free association, also. Either you give me some kind of straight answer, or I'm going to put Clorox in your chardonnay."

"I love you when you're being persuasive," Pietro said. "An answer you shall have. What do I think about all this? Well, if I had to be brief, I would say that I am no Erastian. I will buy the idea that Government in the abstract—what the reformers called the Magistrate and what we call the State—is an institution ordained by God. The Lutherans have a wonderful word for it: They refer to such things as the State, Marriage, the Family as *Schöpfungsordnungen*—ordinances of creation..."

Madeleine interrupted him: "This is being brief?"

"Oh," Pietro said, apologizing. "But what I will not buy is the idea that any particular king, prince, president, parliament or congress is necessarily going to be on God's side. I have always felt that if St. Paul had lived in this twentieth and worst century, he would not have had the benefit of the rose colored glasses he wore when he wrote, in Romans 13:3, 'For rulers are not a terror to good works but to evil.' Personally, I found Hitler distinctly unsettling to good works and alarmingly supportive of evil. And I find Ronald Reagan's Central American policy—not to mention his foreign policy in general and his social policies in particular—far too comforting to a number of people who I happen to consider bad guys. Am I being brief enough?"

"You're not only being brief," Madeleine observed graciously. "You are being clear and forthcoming as well. I take back the part about Clorox in your wine."

"I love it when you encourage me. You want to know what really gets me P.O.'d? It's the fact that turkeys like Ernest Meddlemore can't even see how what they preach blows the Gospel out of the water. They're supposed to be proclaiming the Good News of a Jesus who saved us by being last, lost, least and little—and who, incidentally, got himself executed as a criminal by no less than two Magistracies. But whenever anyone even hints that it might be a nice idea if the government stopped beating up on losers, all they can think of is The Danger To The Government. They run around screaming Law and Order at the little guys when it's precisely the government that's being lawless."

"You believe in civil disobedience then?"

"Believe in it? I've seen it!"

Madeleine glowered: "Watch the archness. You were doing so well without it."

"Ah," Pietro said, mending his ways. "Yes. I do believe in civil disobedience—or to put it more accurately, I think that civil disobedience is justifiable under certain circumstances. The powers that be are ordained of God, and we do indeed need to be subject to their laws for conscience' sake. But when the powers that be themselves become lawless—when they insist upon unconscionable policies and propose to rule by violence rather than law—well then...I say, 'Go for it, baby!' I don't even add the usual pious-pap proviso that you have to be willing to pay the price of your disobedience. The government is very much aware that 'damage should not grow to the hurt of kings'; it will exact the full price of everything you break and then some."

Pietro stopped. "How did I do?" he asked.

"You did wonderfully. No German. No Latin. No fusty reformation names. Just your own nasty thoughts. When we get home, I'll open the *good* chardonnay."

EIGHT

THE BIG BANG

Pietro squeezed the kneaded dough into a snake, rolled it under his hands till it was an even inch in diameter all along and chopped it into one-inch sections. He took a piece, covered the rest, and went to work rolling it out into a paper-thin circle.

Some day he would learn. He had, apropos of yet another Valentine's Day, made the mistake of not jumping the gun on Madeleine. The right way to deal with her was simply to bring home a present—any present. The heart-shaped box of chocolates was not obligatory. Some cheeses, some wursts, even an assortment of tortilla chips, would gladden her heart. Throw in a bottle of decent wine and you were home free. Madeleine loved surprises.

Unfortunately, he never thought of such valentines in time. When the day finally dawned on him and he lamely, if generously, asked her what she wanted, it was too late to avoid the annual suckering in. The conversation was always the same. "What would I like?" she would muse. "Oh, I know. It's Chinese New Year sometime about now, isn't it? Why don't we just stay home and you cook one or two nice little Chinese dishes?"

This gambit—hit upon every year as if she had never thought of it before—invariably produced in him a kind of dreadful resignation. Once she put her mind in an oriental frame, Madeleine was not one to keep things small and simple. Before Pietro could even get the words "beef and oyster sauce" out of his mouth, she was off and running. "How about moo shee pork and pancakes, and something wet to go over rice—yes, I've got it: chicken almond ding—and dry fried string beans with lamb and Szechwan pepper, and…"

She was already up to two-thirds of an afternoon's work for him. Hoping against hope, he said nothing and got, correspondingly, nowhere. "Yum!" she exclaimed. "And don't tell me it's too much food. We'll call up Monica and Mort and make it four. Then we can have scallion pancakes, too. I'll even make the sauces for them. What do you call them in Chinese again?"

"*Choan yow bang*—or *bing,* depending on whose romanization you read," Pietro muttered resignedly. "But since making them shoots an entire afternoon to pieces, I lean toward *bang.* They also require last minute cooking, which is a pain; but for you…"

He went to work immediately, before Madeleine had a chance to realize she hadn't remembered dessert. After he finished the pancakes, or doilies, for the moo shee pork, he addressed himself to the second and, as it were, bigger *bang* for the time and motion buck.

As a matter of fact, though, it was only thinking about them in advance that was heavy; the actual production was downright intriguing. You rolled the dough out thin, brushed it with melted lard, sprinkled it with chopped scallions and maybe a few bacon crumbs, rolled it up jellyroll-style into a long cigarette shape, then coiled it into a spiral, flattened it and chilled it—and then once again rolled it out into a pancake. Just before serving, you browned each one about two minutes to a side in a little oil. The result? Flaky pastry pancakes. With some sauces—hoisin, plum, jao-tze, vinegar, soy, chili paste with garlic and hot sesame oil—even Madeleine's "Yum!" was an understatement.

Working alone though (he had sixteen of the tricky little fellows to produce), he thought of the wonderful and fearful things the human race had come up with as a result of its apparently endless supply of afternoons to kill. How many long Saturdays was it before the scallion *bang* was even hit upon, let alone perfected? Who was the first genius, or clown, who thought of making dough into snakes, snakes into slugs, slugs into circles—and then of applying grease, rolling the circles back into snakes, the snakes back into snails, and the snails back into pancakes?

In strict culinary theory, of course, they were a kind of puff paste: thin sheets of dough with thin layers of fat between them. But to achieve the layering and the thinness by such…well, whimsy: It just proved that at some deep level, human beings never got beyond acting like eleven-year-olds at play.

Legend, in fact, attributed the invention of true puff paste to a French baker's apprentice. The boy had, it is said, forgotten to put butter in the dough when he first mixed it, so in fear and panic he simply wrapped the lump of butter in the dough and rolled and folded and rolled and folded till the evidence of his mistake had vanished. Pietro never thought much of that story. Even if it was fear that first suggested the idea of hiding the butter in the dough, puff paste would never have been perfected without a lot of subsequent fun and games.

The human mind may have been designed in the Divine Image, but it certainly didn't spend too much of its time thinking about God and such things. Far more often, it was out to lunch dreaming of solutions to problems it created purely as a lark. The most bizarre culinary instance Pietro knew of was a Chinese fluffy date pastry which, in addition to the snake/snail syndrome, also involved two distinct doughs, one wrapped inside the other. How many afternoons were dawdled away on that one before...?

On second thought, though, maybe that was what being made in the Divine Image was all about. Eighty percent of all creatures are insects and sixty percent of all insects are beetles. If God was so inordinately fond of beetles, who could fault human beings for playing with paste?

Alas, Pietro thought, half out loud: anybody in his right

mind could. The trouble with eleven-year-old boys was not that they played, but that they didn't know when to stop. And the same was true of the grown men in charge of their destinies; they never, in fact, stopped being eleven-year-old boys. To have whiled away the Saturday afternoons of their lives splitting atoms and fusing nuclei—even to have invented the mushroom-shaped *bang*—all those diversions were no more than the lawful play of creatures made in the image of a God who keeps thinking up beetles. But to have taken those Sabbaths of joyful ease and gone on to abuse them by inventing MIRV's, MX's, and other pre-pubescent contrivances for making pancakes out of people...

"The world," Pietro concluded in full voice, "could use more pastry cooks and fewer politicians. The best and brightest should stop being dim bulbs and make *dim sum* instead. Let them give us valentines that go crunch in the mouth, not St. Valentine's Massacres that leave us splat on the concrete. Let them—"

"What on earth are you babbling about?" Madeleine asked, poking her head in the kitchen. "I hope what you're making turns out lighter than what you're saying. In any case, though, we have to talk about dessert. Any ideas?"

"Only one." Pietro smiled. "Dessert will be your valentine to me. I want fluffy date pastries."

"You'll get ice cream and like it. You're dealing with one eleven-year-old girl who knows what not to start."

NINE

GLUT TO GLORY

Pietro lowered himself carefully onto a kitchen chair. "Do you think," he said to Madeleine, "you could comfort me with a flagon of something that will take my mind off my gluteus maximus? The whole garden is planted. The 'if's and 'and's of your summer eating have been taken care of. My butt, however, will never be the same."

"Serves you right," Madeleine said as she opened the refrigerator. "Nobody told you to plant thirty items in one day. Still, though, I'm surprised. I'd think the sitting apparatus of a writer would be sufficiently developed to be immune to such pains."

She rummaged briefly and announced the results. "You have a choice between old jug wine and new ninety-nine-cent beer. What'll it be?"

"That, my dear, is not a choice; it's a dilemma." Pietro shifted his weight and winced. "Nevertheless, I'll take the beer. Carting off all those stones has made my throat feel like death valley. I have a theory that the previous owner of this place was doing research for Burpee's and succeeded in developing the giant, self-seeding, double hybrid rock. There are twice as many every year."

"Well," Madeleine said, "they don't seem to daunt the veggies much. If last summer was any guide, we're going to be hip-deep in them this time around. You've nearly tripled the size of the garden."

Pietro twisted off the bottle cap, took a long draught and put on a critical look. "I have always felt that the word 'veggies' smacked of regrettable familiarity. God and Mr. Burpee have labored long and hard to provide us with our vegetable loves. A little reverence, please."

"How about a little restraint?" Madeleine shot back. "If it hadn't been for the fuzzy yellow bugs, those zucchini launchers you planted last year would have bombarded the entire neighborhood."

"Nonsense," Pietro said. "There is no such thing as too many zucchini. This year, I shall spray in time and thwart the yellow peril…"

"…and produce the worst glut yet." Madeleine shook her head and poured herself a glass of wine.

"Glut, my love," Pietro said, "is just one more regrettable word. People who use it think they are stigmatizing the abundance of nature. Actually, they betray only the parsimony of their own imaginations. Take zucchini, since you brought them up. Those who cry, 'Hold, enough!' have their minds chained to a single recipe. They boil their squashes to death, drain them insufficiently, add too little butter, and then have the nerve to criticize the Creator for making dull food. They are also lazy about picking them. When God thought up the zucchini, he meant for loving hands to pluck it in the first bloom of its youth. If they insist on trying to eat green dirigibles, they have only the due reward of their sins."

"Glut is glut," Madeleine insisted. "And don't give me the Complete Zucchini Cookbook routine again. Your pasta sauce with cream is a ten, I admit. And the soups are about a seven. But zucchini bread is lucky if it's a one, and zucchini marmalade is off the scale."

"Have you thought of zucchini ice cream?" Pietro asked.

"No, but if you try it, I'm going into the yellow bug breeding business tomorrow."

Pietro sipped his beer and thought. He had always looked on seasonal abundance as one of the great well-springs of cookery. The gardener was forced—no, that was the wrong word—he was *liberated* into inventiveness in the kitchen. Not for him was the enslavement to a single, purist recipe, however good.

If he had an asparagus patch, for example, he could not limit himself simply to buttered asparagus. That might be acceptable to the market-supplied cook who could serve them three times in three months and get away with it. But when one's own supply came all in one week, it was time to have them every day: hot and buttered for openers, of course, but under other sauces, too—and cold as well. And then as sauces in their own right over pasta or eggs—and in omelets, soups, salads, and God only knows what else the oversupplied cook might invent.

The cook with a producing garden was delivered from rhubarb always stewed and spinach always raw. Either would make a pie, an omelet, or a foundation for almost anything else. All it took was a determination to avoid boredom and a willingness to risk the untried. True enough, some eminently forgettable concoctions might now and then result from the enterprise—but then, remembering was not the only part of wisdom.

But, Pietro thought, when you did come up with something memorable, it could stand you in good stead for years to come. Every spring now, he planted onions, leeks, shallots and garlic—whole rows of each—because he had discovered that if he used the plants he thinned out for scallions, he had four different flavors to choose from. Likewise, reasonably tender Swiss chard stems could be cooked like asparagus, either plain or *à la grecque*, and served hot or cold. Lettuces that had started to bolt could be stir-fried with garlic, vinegar and bacon drippings. And New Zealand spinach, at any stage of its indestructible career, could always be thrown into anything.

Seasonal glut was the farthest thing in the world from a curse. Pietro was neither fisherman nor hunter; he lacked the luck for the former and the eyesight for the latter. But he had long ago decided that if a true cook could never have an excess of beets, beans and peppers, neither could too much duck, pheasant, rabbit or venison ever appear in his kitchen. Or mackerel.

Ah, mackerel! The touchstone of the cook who knows

how to turn glut to glory. The season was pretty much over for this year, but it had not passed without Pietro's adding one more triumph to his ever-lengthening list of Things To Do When Yet Another Sackful lands on the porch. He had begun by reteaching his hand its skill with set exercises from seasons past: mackerel in dill sauce, baked mackerel with shrimp sauce, cold mackerel with mayonnaise, mackerel salad, mackerel Breslin-style, poached milt with black butter and capers, broiled roe with bacon and parsley. But still the mackerel came—especially females, bursting with roe second only to shad roe in quality, and absolutely free to boot.

What he had done was sprinkle each pair of roe with lemon juice, salt, and pepper, wrap it in a rasher of very thin bacon, and roll it up in several layers of lavishly buttered phyllo pastry. That, baked in a very hot oven till the pastry was crisp, was the hands-down winner of a decade. The hollandaise he served with the asparagus on the side was sauce for the roe as well, and the combination was pronounced possibly illegal, probably immoral, certainly fattening, and totally good. Pietro smiled to himself.

"What on earth are you grinning about?" Madeleine asked, interrupting his reverie. "I thought you were in pain."

"Only the outward—or downward—man perisheth from excess, my love; the inner cook, having no but to but about abundance, is simply renewed. Tell me. It won't be till fall. But what would you think of leeks in phyllo pastry...maybe with a little cheese mixture folded in as well...?"

TEN

"THERE SHALL BE SHOWERS OF BLESSING"

"Really," Madeleine said, "someone should give her a shower. The baby is due in three weeks."

Pietro, as usual, was caught off guard. Still, he resisted the congenital urge to say, "Who?" The last subject mentioned over breakfast coffee had been repainting the front bedroom. In the forty seconds silence that followed, Madeleine had worked her mysterious mental way from decorating to maternity and simply assumed that her train of thought was as clear to him as it was to herself.

What really worried him was that it was. Living at close quarters with a bona fide thought transmitter made him wonder if he had any brain waves of his own left. She had gone, no doubt, from paint, to blue, to baby boys, to amniocentesis, to Sally, who had just been through the procedure—and from there to crib mattresses, plastic tubs, Peter Rabbit mugs and the lot. Perfectly simple.

He gathered his residual wits and simply acknowledged receipt of the message: "Sally, I presume."

"Of course," she said, totally unsurprised. "Would you be willing to whip up a little Saturday afternoon something for about fifteen women?"

Pietro reflected that being an open receiver wasn't all bad. He had actually heard that particular thought in his mind's ear before Madeleine gave it voice. This time he was ready.

"I do not cook for sexist parties. If male chauvinism is to be banished from polite society, female bonding has to go too. Besides, the shower is one of the more barbaric rituals of the tribe: The hapless girl is seated in an armchair turned into a crepe paper throne and then buried alive in gifts ranging from the cloyingly cute to the practically useless. Not to mention the tastelessly coarse: I understand that some showers can make a bachelor party look like tea with maiden aunts."

"That's only bridal showers," Madeleine said indignantly. "Still, I hate 'women only' just as much as you do. Why don't we put it on a Sunday and make it coed?"

Pietro was aware that he had just been aced. She had passed the question of whether he would cook and was now assuming it was only a matter of when. He decided to give in on both counts and make his last stand on the subject of what.

"Not cocktails, though," he said firmly.

"Why not? It's the easiest kind of party there is."

"It is easy, my love, chiefly because it is not any kind

of party at all. It is a shabby way of chalking off social obligations. Too much booze, no real food, and the bar's closing time announced the minute the guests come in the door. If your heart is set on such rudeness, find yourself another caterer."

"I was just trying to save you work," she said.

Pietro let the transparent falsehood go by. "My work is a gift, gladly given."

"All right, all right," Madeleine interrupted. "Don't get pontifical about it. What do you have in mind instead?"

Pietro could not resist the temptation to reverse the mental telepathy. He thought "Smorgasbord" and occupied ten wordless seconds staring off into the middle distance.

Madeleine came through in full and on time. "Well," she said contentiously, "I just hope that if you do some Swedish thing, you don't make it top-heavy with fish. You get this place smelling like a herring factory."

He smiled. "Me? Never. It just so happens, though, that I do have a small barrel of salt herring and two cans of Swedish anchovies in the outside refrigerator. Let's see: a little plain pickled herring, some herring in wine with dill, some with sour cream and onion, a herring salad…" Pietro was a firm believer in the defensive value of a good offense.

"It's not the herrings I worry about," Madeleine said. "It's the way you dump anchovies into everything else. The last time you did one of these things, it tasted as if you cooked up half the product of the Baltic fishery."

"You exaggerate, my dear," Pietro said soothingly. "I shall keep some dishes totally fishless, just for you. The pot roast, of course, needs a hint of anchovy for authenticity, as do the scalloped potatoes—*Jansson's Temptation*—and the hard-boiled eggs with cream and onions—*Old Man's Hash*. But since you'll want enough food for at least thirty, I'll toss in Swedish meatballs, brown beans, and pickled beets for the non-Scandinavians in the crowd. Plus some Mazarin cakes and a braided saffron bread wreath for dessert."

"It's still an awful lot of fish," she said skeptically. "Put in something else."

"How about steak tartare?" Pietro suggested. "Swedish style, with red onion, egg yolk, finely diced beets and potatoes and lots of capers. Makes a nice presentation. I shall decorate it with tomato roses, scallion flowers, fluted lemon slices and a raw egg yolk in the center."

"Why is it," Madeleine asked, "that Scandinavians can't leave out fish without putting in something raw? Bunch of unreconstructed Vikings."

"You are speaking of my Grandmother's kith and kin," he said testily. "Be respectful, or you will be plundered."

"Promises, promises," she shot back. "Meanwhile, I hope you'll at least try not to turn what started out as a minor party into a Swedish Embassy blowout. Maybe you could make just one thing a little…normal? Why not tomato sauce on the meat balls?"

Pietro stared at her in shock. "Tomato sauce? And to think, I had to hear it from the companion of my bed and board. Wash your mouth out with soap! While I draw breath, not one of my *kött bollar* will ever come within an ocean's width of tomato. Allspice, ginger, nutmeg, beef stock and cream, period. And woe betide the man, woman, or child who even thinks of looking for the ketchup. Leif Erikson must not have died in vain."

"I'm glad I didn't mention oregano," she said, fanning herself. "This shower might have turned out to be my wake."

"Hell hath no fury," Pietro said, "like a Viking scorned. Count your coastlands blessed for that omission."

"Oh thank you, sir," she gushed. "Take a free cow and ten sheep on your way to the boat. Even my daughter. How can I ever thank you?"

"By leaving the menu planning exclusively in my hands," he said airily. "The subject is closed."

"Does that mean no more dishes with fishes?"

"There are promises, my dear, that cannot ever be made, let alone kept. The rest is silence."

He thought *herring savory* and watched Madeleine's face. Nothing.

He thought *anchovy eye:* raw yolk, raw onion, raw anchovies. Nothing again.

He still had brain waves all his own.

He smiled.

ELEVEN

WHAT'S IN A NAME?

Madeleine zapped off the TV set with the remote control switch. "I refuse to look at that dumb name anymore."

"What dumb name?" Pietro asked, looking up from his newspaper.

"Pacific Telesis," she snapped. "It sounds more like a skin disease than a phone company."[6]

"Maybe it's not a phone company. Maybe it's just a Christian punk rock band hiding its light under a bushel."

Madeleine considered the possibility for a moment and discarded it. "Fat chance. Christian music groups always flaunt their Christianity. The bushel has yet to be invented that will cover up the big business of witnessing to Jesus for fun and profit. Not that that isn't a rash in its own right, come to think of it."

"My, my," Pietro observed quietly. "I gather you have

---

6. After its merger in 1997, Madeleine was officially liberated from Pacific Telesis commercials. She now suffers through AT&T commercials instead.

a bone to pick with musical proclaimers of the Gospel."

"You bet I do. I can't stand the way they overlay whatever legitimate musicianship they may have with a lot of commercial sincerity. Listening to them is like snorkeling your way through an ocean of pancake syrup."

"It seems to me that I detect the prejudices of a fifth-generation Episcopalian. These people have to make a living, you know. Outside of you and your mother there isn't all that much of a market for handbells, recorders, and the King's College Choir."

"Can I help it if I was raised to spot corn a mile off? And corn in the name of Jesus halfway across the country? I'm just saying what I think—and what a lot of other people think too, but can't work up the nerve to admit."

"Corn is ever with us, love," Pietro said soothingly. "The beloved nineteenth-century hymnody of your youth was not exactly a seamless tissue of musical spun gold. Besides, the name of Jesus is, I think, quite able to fend for itself despite any or all lapses of taste on the part of its advocates."

"Don't try to soft-soap me," Madeleine huffed. "You squirm your way through those testimonial-ridden performances just as much as I do."

Pietro pondered briefly. "That is true; but permit me to make a distinction. My deepest objections to what is currently called 'Christian music' are rooted not in the tackiness of stretching the safety-net of piety under the supposedly daring highwire act of artistic performance, but in the use of the word 'Christian' to modify *any* human endeavor at all."

"I think you just lost me."

"Be patient and the way will be made plain. First of all, the word 'Christian' appears in Scripture only three times. In its two occurrences in the Book of Acts, it comes from the lips of unbelievers; and in the single reference in 1 Peter, it is used in a way that indicates the writer is at some pains to bestow respectability on it."

"So? How do you get from there to saying there shouldn't be any Christian anything?"

"Quite directly. The word, having had a dubious beginning, has had a history of even more dubious developments. If we are to exalt Christian musicians above all other musicians, why not Christian plumbers above all other plumbers, or Christian chicken-pluckers above their unbelieving but still feather-bedecked fellows? The point, you see, is that music, plumbing and poultry dressing can be—and most properly are—judged by the workmanship, not by the religiosity of their practitioners."

"Hold on, though. Aren't there some activities to which 'Christian' can legitimately be applied? How about Christian parenting, for instance—or Christian marriage?"

"In a word," Pietro said authoritatively, "my answer must be 'No way, Jose'. If you will allow me rather more than a word, though, yet another distinction occurs to me. True enough, there will be Christians who marry and who raise children, just as there will be Christians who unclog sink traps. And truer still, their Christian beliefs may well

impinge on them as they seek to fulfill their roles as part-
ners, parents or plumbers. Nevertheless, the roles themselves (which, mind you, were designed by God when he
created nature, both human and non-human) and—to
come to the point—the performances given by people
who assume those roles, can only be judged by the partic-
ulars of the roles, not by the religion of the role-players."

"Say it simpler."

"A good Jewish mommy is good primarily because of
her mothering, not her religion. A bad Christian plumber
cannot, by reading the Bible more regularly, make amends
for running the sewer line into the dry well instead of the
septic tank."

"Thank you."

"Thank *you. Ergo,* musicians should be judged by their
music, poets by their skill with the language, and stock-
brokers by their ability to recommend companies that do
not go bankrupt. If these people are both Christians *and*
baritones, bards or brokers, we should rejoice that Jesus
has so many competent supporters. If they are good reli-
gionists but poor workmen, we should enjoy their fellow-
ship in the Gospel but take our trade elsewhere. And if
the local Buddhist makes the best pottery…"

"All right, already. But what about the idea that 'the
soul is naturally Christian'?"

"Ah!" Pietro sighed. "So it's Tertullian, is it? *Anima
naturaliter christiana:* the grain of truth that's been used
to justify a ton of half-baked, if not lethal, misrepresenta-
tions of the Gospel. Better just to talk about Jesus and the

Good News; 'Christianity' is mostly a millstone around the neck of the Church."

"But the Church is Christian, isn't it?"

"Nope. It's one, holy, catholic and apostolic. Call it Christian and you close the door on the whole worldful of non-Christians to whom it's sent."

"O...kay. How do you stand on the Christian religion?"

"Negatory. Not only isn't it just for Christians, it isn't even a religion. What Jesus did by dying and rising was the end of whatever religion was trying to accomplish, not the beginning of a new one."

Madeleine sighed. "And just think: all this from just mentioning Christian music."

"What you mentioned," Pietro said archly, "was Pacific Telesis. If your itch for criticism is over, why don't you switch the TV back on?"

TWELVE

PAYING ATTENTION

The dish was one Pietro had eaten the night before in a Thai restaurant. He had scribbled a list of what he judged to be the ingredients and method on the back of a bank deposit slip and was now in the process of reproducing the concoction at his own stove.

> NAM SOD: Shallots and garlic prob'ly fry in a little lard. Then: ground pork, dried chilies, and shredded ginger—cook to evap. but don't brown. Season: fish sauce, lime ju, sugar (bit). Garnish: fresh coriand., shrd. prk skin, red onion, scallion, peanuts. On lettuce. Side: rice.

The grinding, shredding and setting up had already been done. All that was left was to stir-fry everything in order and set it in front of Madeleine for a verdict.

"Close, huh?" he asked as she tried the first mouthful. She said nothing and took a second. Pietro waited. He had learned not to disturb the master at her meditations.

After the fourth taste, she looked up. "Close? It's right on the nose. Isn't there any dish you can't imitate?"

He smiled broadly and tucked into his own portion. It really was close. No pork skin of course, because there wasn't any around; but as far as Madeleine was concerned that was all to the good. For her money, shredded pork skin tasted exactly like rubber bands. She suggested that the only reason the Thais used it for food was that they hadn't yet invented footballs. Still though, how in the world had he known, back there in the restaurant, that it was pork skin?

Paying attention was his answer. In that specific case, attention to other Thai recipes he already knew: Pork skin was one of the commonplaces of the cuisine. But in general, what counted was a settled habit of paying attention to everything your senses and your experiences could tell you.

There were, of course, plenty of things he couldn't imitate. The higher and further reaches of anybody's cuisine defied easy duplication. Talent, after all, was talent. He remembered something he had read once about Nat King Cole's musical arrangements. The writer had said that the difference between them and anyone else's was ultimately mysterious. Somebody could arrange a song for a hundred-piece orchestra, and any A&R man in the country could whip out a piece of music paper and show you how it was done. Cole could set the same piece for piano, bass, and drums, and all you could say was, "How'd he do that?"

Pietro insisted he was only a culinary A & R man; but even at that modest level, paying attention really was everything. If even the talented didn't reach the top without it, how much less the rest of us, whose performances were usually more modest than anything else? For us, it was the principal key to doing something—anything—instead of nothing.

To begin with, it was the line of division between childishness and maturity. Or better said, it was a kind of buffer state between them, a mountainous upland of increasingly concentrated caring that we had to slog through if we were ever to get from green youth to ripe and perfect age. Some of us never made it, of course; and few of us made it all the way. But it remained the defining difference.

The essence of the childish outlook was a delight in results but a deep impatience with the attention to detail needed to achieve them. Pietro's mind went to frozen Chicken Kiev. To packaged poultry stuffing. To instant rice. We were a nation of children, in such a rush for results that we never sat still long enough to master process. And we paid for it with products no adult palate could relish. He drifted to the idea of instant Nam Sod—and popped a circuit breaker in his head.

He thought, too, of the gluing up of preformed plastic kits that now passed for model making. He remembered the models of his youth, and the stiff back he got sitting over a card table pinning wood strips in place for an aeroplane wing. He remembered going on from that to home-designed gliders with six-foot wing spans and perfectly stretched and doped paper skins. Where were the kitless kids of yesteryear? He was obviously getting old.

He'd had a conversation in front of the TV recently with a member of the rising—the oh, so slowly rising—generation. The screen showed someone hand-painting a mayonnaise label on an egg. The youth admired the perfection of the work but went on to insist that it could only be done with a decal. "Even so," Pietro said, trying the path of gentle instruction, "didn't someone, somewhere, have to paint the master decal by hand?" The idea was inconceivable. Pietro felt positively antique; the last man in the world who didn't think Michelangelo bought the Sistine Chapel ceiling in rolls at Pergament.

Still that wasn't entirely fair to the young. By his own definition, the buffer state between inattention and attention wasn't crossed in a day. Those who had pretty well traversed it on one road or another should be patient with those just setting out. The teenager in question might not know from model building, but he had become the master of no mean omelet—and the scourge of any sister who dared to scour his personal, perfectly seasoned iron pan. Where there was fuss there was hope. Maturity was simply a matter of becoming intolerant of inattention.

Besides, there were some roads across that country that we crossed late in the day, or not at all. Models, omelets, and facsimiles of Thai dishes were some of the easier thoroughfares. Attention to people—that perpetual, patient openness to others that was the best definition of love—was a road on which Pietro had not passed as many milestones as he might.

Nor had he passed the ones he did soon enough to prevent disaster. "That was not what I had in mind at all," a certain lady once told him as she walked away from the ditch into which he had driven their relationship. God help him, he had failed to notice. God didn't help though, so the ditch became permanent, a memorial to inattention. The Divine apparently thought it best to leave some lessons as taught. Pietro felt nothing short of ancient.

Madeleine flipped a chopstick across the table at him. "Yoo hoo," she warbled, "I'm still here. Let me see. The first possibility is that you've fallen asleep, but since your head hasn't dropped into the ground pork, I'll rule that out. The next is that you're brooding over the absence of the shredded shoe uppers in the Nam Sod; but it's really perfect without them, so it can't be that. The third is that you're wandering through some of the back alleys of your mind—which is what I thought up till a minute ago. And the last, which I judged by the slightly smitten expression on your face, is that you have finally arrived at the long-slammed door of some old lady friend. How did I do?"

Pietro looked at her in bewildered admiration. "As usual, love, all of the above—and approximately in that order. Come, sit on my lap while I mend my ways."

She came. Why was it when God helped, he always insisted on doing things by one-and-a-halves? Lessons in inattentiveness were one thing. But why a mindreader to give them?

Ah well. The lesson as taught.

"Aren't there," he began, "any thoughts you can't imitate?"

THIRTEEN

CHILDISH THINGS

"You shouldn't get so upset," Pietro complained as he opened the front door of their house. "Henry was just making a perfectly reasonable point with the boy. He's not the monster you're making him out."

Madeleine tossed her coat over the banister. "That's three mistakes in as many sentences," she hissed, squaring off at him. "First, I *am* upset—more by you than by Henry, if you want to know the truth—so knock off the 'shouldn't' and just listen. Second, the point was *not* reasonable. And third, as far as monsters are concerned, there were undoubtedly some nerds who went around claiming Attila the Hun wasn't one either."

Pietro realized too late that he had bitten off a radically indigestible late-night topic. They had just returned from dinner with a couple who had a son, Mark, in his early teens. Their host, who was also the cook for the evening, had gotten into a huff over Mark's refusal even to taste the braised endive. Since neither would give in, the dinner hour degenerated into a Mexican standoff between paternal apoplexy and teenage sullenness.

"Well," Pietro admitted, "it did get a bit sticky there for awhile. But everyone seemed to bury the hatchet, didn't they?"

"They buried it in the kid's head, that's what they did. If they're going to operate like that, they should at least have an honest-to-goodness food fight. A fistful of noodles right in Henry's kisser would've done both him and Mark a lot more good. This way, the poor little guy is just a corked-up bottle of rage."

Unwisely, Pietro tried to gloss over the matter. "Oh, I suppose Henry was a tad extreme. But you've got to admit he had cause. When you've cooked something superb like that, it does go against the grain to have people act as if you're trying to poison them."

"God deliver me from male cooks," she sighed. "You've all got egos that break like eggs and go off like bombs."

"Come on now," Pietro said edgily, "the kid was being an antisocial little brat.

So what if his father picked the wrong time to teach him manners. He was just asking for it. What's Henry supposed to do? Bow meekly before the tyranny of half-formed taste?"

"Oh, wow!" Madeleine said archly. "Now it comes out. Misery loves company, eh?"

"As you well know," Pietro shot back, "I am very patient with the strange eating habits of your children.

So let's keep this little…discussion…in focus. You really think Henry was totally wrong?"

"Yes."

"*Totally?*"

"I already answered that."

"He had no right at all to be incensed at such rudeness?"

"None."

"Well then," Pietro sighed, "perhaps you will enlighten me as to just what he did have right…"

"I will," she broke in; "but only if you get that 'I must deal gently with the feebleminded' tone out of your voice. Condescending when you're wrong just makes you wronger—and don't correct my English, either."

Pietro simply waved her to proceed.

"There are three subjects," she said in her best teacher's voice, "on which the human race is stark staring bonkers: religion, sex and eating (including drinking). The only subject that's worse is trying to reform other people's attitudes toward them at the dinner table."

"Even if those other people are half-cocked teenagers?"

"Especially if they are," she snapped. "Teenagers have one major campaign going on in their lives, and that's the sorting out of who in the world they are. Since religion, sex and food are practically the closest things to their identity, the chances are they'll disagree with their parents' attitudes on all three, just so they can be sure they're breathing on their own."

"That pardons bad manners?" Pietro asked.

"It's not a question of pardon. It's just a matter of accepting delivery on what you signed up for. Henry didn't have to have children, but once he did, he's stuck. To expect teenagers not to reject their parents' cooking is about as reasonable as expecting babies not to wet their pants."

"But if nobody trains them to care," Pietro said, "how are they going to learn?"

"That's up to them in the long run. All I know is that your enthusiasm for shoving uplift down everybody's throat gives me the willies—besides being a lot of malarkey. Very few kids who get old enough to reach their wedding night have a problem with enuresis. And even fewer thirty-five year olds with a walletful of credit cards have trouble getting through dinner at Lutece."

"But I was raised to eat everything. It never did me any…"

Madeleine cut him off. "All I can say is, you have a short memory. You mean there wasn't anything your parents ever tried, and failed, to get you to eat?"

"Well, there were eggs, of course, and cooked green pepper…and fish—though I did like the taste of plain cod liver oil."

"Terrific! Talk about kids who could drive parents up the wall!"

"Now that you mention it," Pietro reflected, "they just laughed and threw up their hands."

"Thank you," Madeleine said elaborately. "Now. The next time you see Henry, why don't you simply tell him your life's story?"

FOURTEEN

ON THE HOT SEAT

"It was just a businessmen's lunch," Pietro said as offhandedly as he could, trying to get off the subject.

"Businessmen's lunches are never *just,*" Madeleine shot back. "In fact, as far as wives are concerned, they're completely *un*just. You luck out with no work and all play while I get noon to three in solitary without even a yogurt. Where'd you eat, at Lutece or The Palace?"

Pietro made the mistake of trying to humor her. "Neither," he said. "Henry and I were so busy doing deals, we only had time for a *Sabrett's.*"[7]

"Try again," she said menacingly. "I want the truth!"

"Well, actually, it was an Indian restaurant. But not all that good really. I'd give it a 2 on a scale of 10."

"Spare me the details of your suffering. I haven't had any kind of Indian food in years. For your penance, you have to cook me some. Besides, hot weather calls for spicy food."

---

7. An infamous New York hotdog.

75

He couldn't resist his lifelong habit of countering pressure with delay. "All right," he said. "But only if you can prove your last assertion rationally."

"What? I have to pass some kind of test before I get simple justice?"

"If you want justice, find a judge. If you want an Indian dinner, take it on the cook's terms. Not afraid of a little quiz, are you?"

"Just try me," she said, narrowing her eyes. "Incidentally, you wouldn't be afraid of a little side bet, would you?"

"How do you mean?"

"If there are things about hot food that I know and you don't, you owe me another whole Indian dinner for each one."

Pietro gulped a "Very well" and asked his first question: "What makes spicy food hot?"

"That's easy," she said. "Chili peppers."

"To what botanical genus do they belong?"

"Genus *Capsicum*," she answered. "Do *you* happen to know what family they belong to?"

"Of course," he said. "Nightshade."

"Botanical name?" she asked.

"Er…"

"*Solanaceae!*" she exclaimed. "Two dinners for me! Don't mess with a botany major."

Pietro tried to regroup his forces. "What is the relation of chili peppers to, say, black pepper?"

"Black pepper, or *Piper nigrum*, is the true pepper. The capsicums are a whole 'nother kettle of chilies."

"Very funny," he sneered. "Are you saying, then, that all the so-called capsicum peppers are hot?"

"No. The *Capsicum grossum,* or ordinary bell pepper, is mild. So are the varieties called 'pimiento'—witness the European paprikas, for example. By the way can you spell 'pimiento'?"

"Easy," he said, "p-i-m-e-n-t-o."

"Wrong!" she crowed. "Pimento without the 'i' is allspice. Three dinners for me! Isn't this a fun test? More, more!"

Pietro decided to give botany a wide berth. "Why are hot peppers used so extensively in the cuisines of hot climates?"

Madeleine marshaled her thought. "Well, to begin with, the granddaddy of all garden peppers, *Capsicum frutescens,* is from the tropics. Cooks who lived there simply used what was at hand."

"That is not an answer, it is just a restatement of my question with the 'why' chopped off. Do better or you fail the test."

"You mean the passing grade is a hundred?"

"Precisely."

"But you never said…"

"You never asked. Answer the question."

Madeleine decided she had played this fish long enough. It was time to reel him in. "Having audited your course before," she said smoothly, "I believe the answer you want is either the old bromide about peppers making your system so hot that the weather seems mild by comparison, or else the half-truth that they cause perspiration which, in turn, cools you by evaporating in the breeze."

"Why is the latter a half-truth?"

"What if there's no breeze?"

Pietro sensed a trap, but couldn't spot it. "I take it you're saying there is a connection between peppers and perspiration, but there's more to it than evaporation."

"Precisely," Madeleine parodied him. "Do you by any chance know what that connection is?"

"Er..."

"Want a hint?"

"Well..."

"It's got to do with vitamins," she said. "What have peppers got lots of?"

"Vitamin C?" he guessed.

"Excellent! Now what has vitamin C got to do with perspiration?"

"Er..."

"It's water soluble and gets carried away when you sweat. Peppers replace what they make you lose—and ripe, red ones replace twice as much as green.

"Four dinners for me! What other vitamins are water soluble?"

"Er..."

"The B complex. Five dinners! And what is a particularly refreshing hot-weather source of B vitamins?"

"Er..."

"Yogurt. Six dinners! And in what cuisine do both hot peppers and yogurt play major roles?"

"Indian!" he shouted. "Stop! You pass."

"Thank you," she said quietly. "A whole week's worth of Indian food would have been a bit much."

FIFTEEN

BETWEEN PACIFISM AND WAR

Madeleine laid the letter on her sewing table and turned off the TV.

"Hey, no fair," Pietro complained. "The family of giggly blondes was about to win the double dinette set if they could explain the difference between Boy George, George Fox, and Foxy Grandpa."

"Tough," Madeleine said. "That letter was from Dominique. They're having problems with Timmy."

"What kind of problems could a clean-cut kid like your sister's son possibly have? What'd he do? Flunk out of a Frosted Mini-Wheat commercial?"

"No. He claims he's a pacifist. His father is so furious he's about to tell him to go live someplace else. Dominique's caught in the middle, as usual. I want you to talk to me about it but I don't want you to get into your usual lather over the fact that she and Victor are born-again Christians."

"Hmmm," Pietro said, canceling several trains of critical thought. "Does that mean I *am* allowed to make latherless comments about your sister's family's religio-political proclivities? I hope so, because it seems to me that your brother-in-law's desire to kick his son out in the cold is not entirely separable from his 'God is not mocked' theology and his 'God bless America' politics."

"I suppose," said Madeleine. "But just don't start in on Victor."

Pietro suppressed a snappy riposte. "I begin," he said pointedly, "with only two headings, Pacifism and War—and with absolutely no foam at my mouth. There! What do you think so far?"

"I think you've said almost nothing."

"But you must admit I've said it very calmly."

Madeleine glared at him. "Get *on*!"

This was a temptation Pietro failed to resist. "Someday, my dear, you must explain to me why 'getting *on*' is commanded and 'starting *in*' is forbidden."

Madeleine exploded at him. "Someday I'll tell *you* to get out. Stop with the everlasting verbal fencing and say something!"

"Fine," Pietro said, repenting. "Pacifism first. If people are pacifists for the simple reason that they'd rather die than fight, then as far as I can see, they can always justify their position by saying that's exactly what Jesus did. Not only that, but they can bear witness to the ultimate truth that God saves the world by losing rather than winning, by dying rather than living. But if they are pacifists because they think pacifism will be an effective program for talking a war-like world out of its hostilities, they haven't got a leg to stand on. Because that's just not how it happens. Put a pacifist in the way of a determined warmonger, and you don't get a converted warmonger; you get a dead pacifist. So as a sacrament of the mystery of redemption, pacifism is great; but as a gimmick for stopping wars, it's hopeless."

Madeleine interrupted him. "In her letter, Dominique sent along a piece that Timmy wrote. He says people like you underestimate the power of pacifism's good example."

"Ever since Adam and Eve, my dear, the power of good example has been so low it can't possibly be underestimated. Jesus gave the world the best example it ever saw and the world's nastiness quotient wasn't in the least affected by it. Timmy is what, eighteen? At eighteen you're impressed by statements like, 'If everyone was a pacifist, wars couldn't happen'. But as you get older you find such arguments no more to the point than, 'If everyone had perfect pitch, tone-deafness would be impossible'. Their logic is unassailable but their major premise just isn't screwed down to the real world."

"Still, though," Madeleine pressed, "you're not saying he *shouldn't* be a pacifist, are you?"

"Absolutely not. Pacifism is a sacrament of the mystery—a *real presence* of it, if you like. Even if Timmy becomes a pacifist for all the wrong reasons, his pacifism will still be, *in fact*, a way of union with Jesus. It will also, of course, still remain a flop as a device for stopping war."

"What *about* war, though? Dominique says Victor thinks it's absolutely a Christian duty for Timmy to run out and fight for his country any time the President says 'sic 'em, boys'."

Pietro put on his best defense attorney manner. "Let the record show that the prosecution was the first to start in on poor Victor."

"You never give up, do you?" growled Madeleine.

"I guess I don't. My personal vocation falls somewhere *between* pacifism and war. If I had to put a name on it, I would say I am called to irenic belligerence. Nevertheless, I have some grave reservations about unvarnished war enthusiasts like Victor. Maybe a very long time ago they could make out a case for a 'just war'. Certainly plenty of Christians once thought they could. But a lot of things have changed since then, and war itself is one of them. In the old days—maybe even right up until the middle of this century—war could be viewed as an instrument of political policy. You know: It was rough and messy to have to blow up all those cities and people, but it stopped Hitler and gave the world another crack at life and freedom. But ever since we opened up the possibility of nuclear war, that kind of talk became irrelevant. Any considerable nuclear exchange will leave us with nothing to attach a policy to and no bearable life to be free for. So for my money, it adds up like this: Victor is nuts; but since he's no nuttier than the whole system, who's to say whether he's crazy or I'm sane? The best we're going to do—what we have done, in fact, for forty years—is fight a lot of old-style, two-bit wars and hope they don't escalate into a newfangled non-war to end all."

"You have nothing to say about the Christian Position?" Madeleine asked.

"Nothing."

"No advice as to which course Timmy or Victor should take?"

"None."

"This is not like you."

"Ah, but it is," Pietro said. "My firmest secular opinion is that, by Murphy's Law, we will sooner or later blast ourselves and the whole world straight into the howling agony of Jesus' passion and death. And my devoutest belief is that when we get there—pacifists and Pentagon generals alike—we will all be safe in the power of his resurrection. Put the two together and you get no advice, just, 'Hang on, the *terrible* goodness is about to take over'."

"Well!" Madeleine remarked.

"*Well* isn't exactly the word," Pietro said. "Try, *terrific,* with an accent on the *terr.*"

SIXTEEN

EATING OUT

"If you insist on wearing those ratty painter's pants to Harry's cookout," Madeleine declared, "I'm staying home."

Pietro feigned surprise. "What? You mean hammer loops and ruler pockets are no longer 'in'? I shall change immediately."

He went into the closet and rummaged. "Let me see. Where did I put my Brooks Brothers' two-button caveman costume and my Abercrombie and Fitch Alley Oop club? That'd be just the outfit."

"And…" Madeleine added menacingly, "if you don't get all the anti-barbecue pronouncements out of your system before we leave here, you'll be sorry I came along."

"That's a tall order," he said. "Perhaps if I do a little primal screaming…"

"Oh, come on. Cookouts are not that bad. Just put on something sensible and let's go. We're late already."

"The only sensible thing to wear to one of Harry's evening sacrifices is a fireman's mask and air tanks. The whole ritual is retrogressive. It took humankind 50,000 years to figure out how to dine without breathing smoke, and here we are, the flowers of civilization, checking our digital watches to make sure we can climb back into the cave on time."

"Did it ever occur to *you* that maybe you're the throwback? Everybody goes to barbecues and loves them."

"Everybody went to public hangings, too. The presence of a crowd is no proof that the sunny side of human nature is being addressed."

"Bosh!" she said, trying to end the discussion. "God made the great outdoors.

"If he doesn't object to open-air dining, why should you?"

"Aha!" Pietro exclaimed. "The oldest, shabbiest rhetorical trick in the book: when the argument is weak, hang it in the Divine. I simply cannot let that pass."

"Don't then. Just start dressing."

"Very well," he said, changing his shirt. "You refer to the apparent absence of supernatural objection to cookouts..."

"What do you mean, *apparent*? Where in the Bible does it say, 'No barbecues'? In my book, silence gives consent."

"Not quite. If you mean that God made no commandment against eating a cow a la charcoal-lighter off paper plates with plastic forks, I concede your point.

But then, he also issued no proscription against putting bananas in your ears."

"What has that got to do with anything?"

"It would seem that the Ruler of the Universe expects human good sense to avoid certain obviously unattractive excesses on the one hand…"

"Oh, I see," she interrupted. "Like those painter's pants. Don't forget to change them, too."

Pietro ignored her. "…and, on the other, to eschew certain unnecessary cruelties."

"Cruelties?"

"Yes. The sufferings a true cook undergoes while attending a barbecue are beyond description, let alone analysis."

"But you'll try both, won't you?"

"Naturally. Just listen. Those who commit cookoutery fall into two classes. The first is the category of the totally incompetent—of those who haven't the foggiest notion when anything is done to any degree whatsoever and who therefore produce only two kinds of steak: raw or vulcanized."

"That's your idea of cruelty?"

"Go ahead and mock. Only those who have suffered know. Nevertheless, the other class of cookoutery is more cruel still. This is the category of the four-star, cordon bleu *maitre des pits*, who turns the simple business of grilling a steak into a production that makes the royal wedding look like two teenagers in the county courthouse. Such processions of food! Such ritual laying of fires! Such boring recitals of marinade ingredients! Such…"

"At least that kind produces decent steaks, though, right?"

"Yes. But what good is competence if it hasn't the sense to present its product in a proper setting? Eating a perfectly grilled steak in a backyard full of children, dogs and flies—and devoid of anyplace to stand your wine glass while you cut your meat—is like…is like…"

"Don't stop now," Madeleine urged, "you'll make it."

"…is like doing needlepoint on Kleenex…"

"Come, come. You can do better than that."

"…it's like putting the Sistine Chapel ceiling in a rumpus room…"

"Better. Try once more."

"…it's like installing the windows of Chartres in an airline toilet…"

"That's just reaching. What exactly are you trying to get at?"

"Only that perfection should be presented in a context of equal perfection."

"Oh. Why didn't you say so? What you mean is it's like taking me to a party while you're still wearing painter's pants. Thank heaven you saw the light! Finish changing. I'll start the car…"

SEVENTEEN

"NONE IS SO BLIND"

The meal was putting a strain on Pietro's honesty. The host had scorched the tomato sauce during manufacture and the hostess had managed, through two supererogatory rounds of martinis, to boil the pasta almost to jelly. When they insisted on eliciting his comments, Pietro tried to get by with a mumbled "excellent," but the word-for-all-work betrayed him. He lacked the teenager's flair for suffusing it with cosmic significance. He had to ask for seconds to lift the curse of his faint praise.

Still, it wasn't enough. What they needed was some unsolicited enthusiasm from him, so he resolved to hail the dessert, no matter what. "Marvelous," he sang out as the pie appeared; "I love raspberry chiffon."

He should have known better. The company did a quick double take and broke down in laughter. He had meant only to reassure his hosts, but for the tenth or twentieth time in his life, he had walked into the trap that invariably destroyed his own credibility: The chiffon, they informed him, was lime: bright, unmistakable, poison-green lime. Pietro was color-blind.

There followed the usual five minutes' worth of uncomprehending, half-gloating curiosity he had put up with all his life. No, his perceived world was not like Woody Allen's *Manhattan,* at least not in hue: He was only slightly red-green blind. Yes, he could deal with traffic lights: The red looked like orange and the green was mostly blue. Anyway the stop light was always on top. He left unmentioned some other problems: He could hardly tell the red from the yellow, or the green from a mercury-vapor street lamp—and, ever since some bureaucrat changed the stop signs from yellow to red, he sometimes didn't see them at all against green foliage.

But his life wasn't the black and white movie they imagined. His blue jays were as blue as the next fellow's and his lemons the same yellow that was a metaphysical experience shared by all. Things were really bad only in childhood when five-year-old cousins took to rolling on the floor in heartless mirth at the uncoordinated colors of his ties and shirts. He solved the problem by coding his clothes numerically. Once he had given up the idea of being either a surgeon or a cable-splicer, he lived happily ever after. Except, of course, for the odd chiffon pie.

"But how can you cook," they asked, "if you can't see colors?" Pietro had been down this blind alley before; the best course was to say nothing. Those who took relish in seeing the mighty fall would hardly be interested in learning how, in fact, his color-blindness almost never tripped him up in the kitchen (stay away from pastel icings and you're home free). And those who were honestly curious might not have the patience to hear the answer out. He tapped his forehead knowingly. "Many tricks of the trade," he said.

He tucked into the pie. Having as usual, forgotten whether it was red or green, he hoped that his palate would come to the aid of his eyesight. But it did not. The taste, lying somewhere between room deodorant and spray polish, was no help. He ate in what he trusted looked like a canny silence.

Privately, he would be the first to admit the culinary drawbacks of working without a piece of sensory equipment. He could never use redness or greenness as his only test. And the difficulty was, if anything, compounded by the slightness of his affliction. He could see most reds and greens, but he could never anticipate the occasional ones that confused him.

There was, for example, the dinner party at which he had served three whole heads of cauliflower. He had made the mistake of steaming them in an aluminum pot. Their color, about which curious remarks were made, depressed him. He assumed all evening they were a light elephant gray. Only later did someone ask him for his secret of making cauliflower shocking pink.

Red wines were a problem, too. He had trouble, oddly, spotting the brownish tinge in wine that was over the hill due to excessive oxidation. Still, though, the burnt taste came through clearly enough, so it wasn't a total loss.

In fact, it was just that marvelous redundancy of the senses that was the key to working one's way around the limitation. What the eye couldn't see, the nose would grasp in an instant. Try as he might, Pietro could never have decided whether his host's tomato sauce had a brownish cast to it; but he had picked up the telltale scent of caramelization the minute the lid came off the dish.

And what the nose couldn't assess, some other sense could. Lamb and beef were brought to perfect pinkness not by perceiving their color but by gauging the temperature of the inside of the roast with a metal skewer tested against the lip (if it's red hot, you've just ruined twenty dollars worth of meat). Steaks were done when the finger felt them properly springy. And green vegetables?

Ah, green vegetables. For what conceivably might have been his nemesis, Pietro invariably received nothing but compliments. The reason? The same that enabled Beethoven to compose after he was deaf: The mind could manage to interpret even what the sense refused to report.

Pietro had, he supposed, never seen the true differences between the various greens with which the Creator had endowed his creatures of bush and vine; but it didn't matter. With a little loving care, they were all enhancible by any cook who took the trouble to learn what was involved.

Green beans, for example, had to be cooked quickly, without a cover, and then shocked under the cold tap to set them. No putting them on in cold water and sucking the color out while you dragged them up to heat: just a sudden plunge, all at once, into boiling water, and the fastest possible return to the boil. And no lid: All the cover did was condense back into the pot the volatile acids that vitiated the greenness. The old cooks who put baking soda in the beans had the right principle but the wrong implementation. The alkalizing effect made them green indeed, but the soda also produced a mushy texture and an off taste. No color was worth that sacrifice.

Perhaps, Pietro thought, he overcompensated for his color-blindness by cooking everything to the tooth; but since his methods assured both texture and tint, it was all to the good. And the bonus did not end there. Green vegetables, undercooked to start with and then cooled quickly, were not only a delight to eye and mouth; they were also a boon to the cook on a tight schedule. All they needed at the last minute was to be reheated in a bath of melted butter and seasoned to taste.

The only remaining problem for the color-blind cook turned out to be no problem. Arranging foods tastefully on a plate required next to no color perception at all. God was kinder than the manufacturers of shirts and ties. Any vegetable, cooked knowledgeably to retain its true color, looked good next to anything else. All you needed was a simple sense of contrast: Potatoes and cauliflower called for something dark (say, spinach) between them, broccoli and green beans for something light (say, carrots). Just alternate your items—except with beets, which could go anywhere because they ended up everywhere.

He smiled, to himself. There was a way around every difficulty—even, no doubt, the vexing question of the lime pie...

He stopped smiling.

...or was it raspberry?

EIGHTEEN

CRASH LANDING

Pietro marched in from the garden with a six-quart pot full of basil leaves.

"There," he said, depositing it with a flourish in front of Madeleine. "I cut both rows of plants back hard; that should slow down the little over-achievers for awhile. If you'll pick off the stems, I'll stuff the leaves in sandwich bags and freeze them—except of course for what I need for supper."

She glowered at him. "Pesto? Again? You're going to turn us all green before summer is out. Why do you always plant so much basil?"

"Because, my love, it produces your favorite color and my favorite dish. I'll make you a deal, though. Bear with me tonight, and I'll promise you no more pesto for two weeks. It's a crime, of course, committing pesto-cide right in the middle of the season. But for you..."

He ducked her punch and fetched the Asiago and

the shelled Brazil nuts. Chopping the cheese coarse and smashing the nuts with the flat of a cleaver, he tossed both into the blender. Ever since OPEC, or somebody, had raised the price of pine nuts to just under that of diamonds, he'd been experimenting. Walnuts, the usual substitute, were too aggressive. Brazils, he discovered, took more gracefully to the strictly supporting role the nuts were supposed to play.

He peeled and smashed some garlic cloves, punched the blender to grind, added the garlic and poured in enough olive oil to get the whole mixture flowing easily. After that it was just basil leaves to color and salt to taste, plus a splash of hot water at the end to bring everything together smoothly. This, he felt, was real cooking: A good dish had to be *tuned*, like a guitar. It was the senses in free experiment, not the mind chained to a recipe, that reigned over the process. The only thing you had to avoid was chopping up bits of rubber spatula along with the basil.

The phone rang. Madeleine answered it and put on a dark green look. She laid her hand over the receiver and widened her eyes derisively.

"It's dear, sweet Linda, and she has some terrible problem she just has to talk to Pietro about. Predatory female! The next time she snuggles up to you, I'll scratch her eyes out."

Pietro was tempted to say something lighthearted about the unsatisfactoriness of telephonic snuggling when one's wife was sitting three feet away, but he had learned long ago not to rattle tigresses' cages. Instead, he simply waited in silence until she cut Linda off with an imperious "Here; you may tell him." She passed the phone, holding it by the cord as if she were dangling a dead rat. Madeleine was nothing if not clear about her feelings.

After a few carefully unendearing pleasantries, Pietro settled down to listening. Linda, it seems, had forty people coming for a buffet in two hours. She had made ten quarts of turkey à la king last night, but when she took it out of the refrigerator just ten minutes ago it looked a little funny on top. Did Pietro think it was all right?

"How do you mean, funny?" he asked clinically.

"Sort of...well, foamy," she replied

Pietro sighed. "Linda, how did you store it overnight? I know you had it in the refrigerator, but what did you put it in?"

"In a twelve-quart pot with a lid."

Pietro sighed again. "Linda, I want you to do something instructive. Can you reach the pot from where you are?"

She said yes, so he proceeded. "Touch the outside of the pot. It's nice and cold, isn't it? Now roll up your right sleeve, if any, and plunge your hand into the very middle of the mixture. Describe, please, what you feel."

She gasped. "Why, it's warm! Toasty warm."

"Not toasty-warm, my dear. We in the food business refer to that as festery-warm. You have ten quarts of incipient food-poisoning there; Lucretia Borgia could have taken lessons from you. Unfortunately, however, our times are not hers; if you serve it, you'll get twenty-five to life in the slammer for mass murder."

"But how did that happen?" she whimpered.

"Unbrowned sauces have to be cooled rapidly. You should have put that stuff in three or four separate pots—without covers. Don't feel bad, though. You've made some bacteria very happy."

Pietro glanced at Madeleine. The conversation so far had done wonders for her appearance. Glower and menace were gone: The surmised prospect of Linda headed for terminal despair had put a serene smile on her face. Pietro decided he could risk a more consoling tone.

"But don't worry, love," he said, "all is not lost."

"You mean, there's something I can do with it? Oh, thank goodness."

"Well, to be truthful, the only thing you can prudently do with what you've got is dump it, wash the pot and make something else. Linda? Linda? Are you there?"

He waited for her to respond and then continued. "Now Linda, what you must not do is panic. Think of yourself as Karen Black in *Airport '77*. I can't guarantee that Charlton Heston will drop in through the ceiling; but if you will treat your kitchen as the cockpit of a crippled 747, I think I can talk you safely down. Just do exactly what I tell you, and report back to me. What's that? No, Linda, I am not going to give you a recipe. You are going to do something called *cooking*—with nothing more than your own wits and what you've got on hand. I know it's scary. But you can do it, girl, you can do it. Ready?"

She snuffled something incomprehensible, so he forged ahead. "Go to the pantry, Karen—I mean, Linda—and bring out all the pasta you can find. It's the stiff, creamy yellow stuff in those long, flat boxes."

"I've got it," she said, "but it's all different shapes—and lots of half-boxes."

"No matter," he reassured her. "How much would you say you had altogether?"

"About five pounds," she answered quickly.

"Good girl. You're going to make it." He ran her through a checklist. Canned tomatoes? Affirmative: two cans. Cheeses? Yes, all scraps, but lots: Jarlsberg, cheddar, cottage, Romano, sliced provolone, cheez-whiz... "My God, girl, keep your hands off the cheez-whiz. You nearly blew it." Meats? Yes, good: salami, pepperoni, meat loaf, two pork chops and five chicken wings. Liquids? Fine: sour cream, yogurt, milk, cream, white wine. Seasonings? Right on: oregano, red pepper, salt. "By George, Linda, I think you've done it. You're ready to bring her in. We're going to lose radio contact any minute now, so listen closely and..." Pietro paused so he could work up the requisite sob. "And...good luck, doll."

Suddenly, he was all business again.

"Dump turkey à la regicide. Wash pot. Boil ten quarts water. Add salt. Boil pasta four minutes. Drain. Return to pot. Set oven at 375° and cut up everything you can into chunks. Add to pot. Throw in liquids till it's nice and runny. Add seasonings till it tastes emphatic. Mix it all up

101

with both hands, cover and put in oven for one hour or until…"

Pietro hit the off button on the phone and collapsed dramatically on the table. "Let's pray for her Madeleine," he said in exhaustion. "It's out of our hands now."

After a minute he put the phone back on its base and beamed. "I didn't tell her, love, but that actually is a recipe. It's called *Pasta à la Summer Cottage Close-out,* or *How To Empty Out A Fire Island Larder On Labor Day.* Not exactly Escoffier, I admit. But then, he didn't give lessons in refrigerator cleaning. None of us is perfect."

NINETEEN

"THERE ARE SOME THINGS I WILL NOT EAT"

"I suppose I should be ready for it by now," Madeleine complained, "but I never am. What gets into you around your birthday every year that makes you force a dinner of boiled tongue on me? You *are* aware you do that, aren't you?"

"Now that you mention it, I guess I am," Pietro replied. "It's only fair, though. After all, *you* get to have the last word on at least ninety-five percent of the menus here."

"But *tongue!* You know I can't stand it. Yecch!"

"Oh, come now. If you'd just concentrate on the flavor, it wouldn't bother you so much. You like other smoked meats."

"How can anyone think about flavor with something like that lying on the platter? You can see the taste buds, for crying out loud—not to mention the roots, or whatever, where it was attached. Couldn't you at least trim it somehow—carve it into a block so people wouldn't have to think about what it was?"

Pietro sighed. Each year, he hoped that twelve months without tongue would somehow mitigate her aversion to it, but it never did. She went through the same post mortem on the meal anyway. And he responded with the same unavailing arguments.

"What's the point of trying to disguise it? It's just beef. You don't trim a rib roast so it looks like a loaf of bread, do you?"

"No. But tongue is different."

"Why? Because it's been in somebody's mouth? A rib roast was in somebody's side, if you think about it. And an eye of the round was in somebody's rump."

"Look. We've been through all this before. Instead of trying to convert me, why don't you try to understand? You're supposed to be the great arguer on any side of any question. If you can't see my point, the least you could do is put yourself in my position and think a little."

"You want *me* to make an argument for hating tongue? That's silly. I've loved it all my life—served whole, too, at the table. I never even thought it was a problem until you had fits."

"So think now. I just know there's a good reason somewhere."

Pietro gave in. "Well, all right. But you have to help by thinking with me. Let's begin by refining the question. Since you're not a vegetarian, we're not discussing squeamishness about meat in general, right?"

"Right."

"Good. So we must be talking about certain kinds of meat. Could it be that you find muscle meats acceptable and that you have problems only with organ meats?"

"No. I like liver. And also tripe when you fix it in a red sauce."

"Hmm. I was going to make a case that it was the texture of organ meats that put you off. Between liver and tripe, though, you've got me stopped: One's soft, the other's rubbery. By that token, however, how come you hate kidneys? Sautéed briefly, they're springy; stewed to death, they're tender. What's the difference?"

"You're supposed to be telling me, remember?"

"Oh, yes. Well, if it's not texture, let's try flavor. Kidneys sometimes taste a bit…strong, if you know what I mean. What do you say to that as an explanation?"

"No good. I dislike them even when they're mild."

"Okay. Let's try another tack. Answer me a series of questions. How do you feel about sweetbreads?"

"I can take them or leave them."

"Heart?"

"I'd rather leave it."

"Brains?"

"Gack!"

Pietro sat back in his chair and reflected for a moment. "I think, Madeleine, that I see the root of your problem. Just to be sure, though, let me ask three more questions—this time about regular meats, not innards. How does the thought of eating feet strike you?"

"Not very well, thank you."

"And what about tails?"

"If I know they're being served, I can't get them down."

"And ears?"

"Double gack!"

"Ah, yes," Pietro said, touching his finger tips together. "Just as I thought. You are suffering from an attack of the pathetic fallacy: Your mind, when it thinks of animal parts—particularly of *whole* parts—cannot avoid thinking of human counterparts. For you, the thought of a cow's tongue leads directly to apprehension about the safety of your own—and so on down the line: brains, hearts, feet, ears, the lot. Since you take them all personally, you find yourself horrified at the thought of their being eaten. I, on the other hand, having no such hang-up, enjoy them mightily. There! How's that for an understanding?"

"Not bad. The only things it doesn't explain are why I should take an ox's tail personally when I haven't got one of my own to worry about—and why you, who claim to take nothing personally, refused to eat prairie oysters at that barbecue in Montana."

"Oh…well…there *are* limits."

"Aha! So you *do* take some things personally, eh?"

"One or two, I suppose. But really…"

"Stop right there. *That's* an understanding. And just to show you how understanding I am, why don't you buy yourself a tongue for your birthday? I'll have the leftover chicken that's in the fridge."

TWENTY

UNCLE STURDY'S GHOST

"Now you owe me," Madeleine said as she hung up the phone. "Gina and Harry are coming here for Thanksgiving. Since I just got you out of having to drive to Jersey, I get to decide what we serve. Right?"

Pietro knew an inevitability when he heard one, but the suggestion that he bow to it on command nettled him. He decided to be difficult.

"If you say so, my love," he began blandly. "I'm sure if you mail the menu to Gina today, she'll have plenty of time to figure out how to cook everything in Paterson and keep it hot all the way here. Of course, if I were asked, I might just be willing to cook the dinner myself. That way you'd be spared your sister's specialties: cauliflower in Elmer's glue, Brussels sprouts *à la mush*, *pommes de terre aux lumps*, and apple pie with Naugahyde crust."

"Let me know when you're through," Madeleine said, refusing to be roped in.

"I have often wondered," Pietro rambled on, "how she manages to find Naugahyde of such surpassing toughness. I mean, your average car seat or TV recliner wears out in a year or so. One of Gina's top crusts could last a decade. My theory is that she uses only the hide of the fierce New Jersey Nauga—a beast that must be hunted along the fetid banks of the Passaic by the light of a waning gibbous moon."

Madeleine drummed on the table with her fingers. "All right," she said. "Consider yourself asked. I still pick the menu."

"Some day," Pietro said archly, "you might show me your diploma from the Ayatollah Khomeini Correspondence School of Diplomacy. *O tempora! O mores:* My great uncle, Sturtevant Hodding Sturtevant III, late of the State Department, would no doubt turn over in his grave if he saw me capitulating to such ham-fisted tactics; but then…" Pietro paused for a sigh… "I suppose there's nothing for it but to accept…"

"If your great uncle could see you, he wouldn't have a grave to turn over in," Madeleine crowed. "But thanks anyway for the capitulation."

"Don't thank me yet. As I was about to say before you interrupted, I accept, with the proviso that we discuss your proposed menu in reverse order: dessert first, side dishes next, entrée last."

"I don't like the sound of that," she said, squinting at him. "You'd better not try any tricks."

Pietro put his hand to his breast and closed his eyes

piously. "As Uncle Sturdy is my witness, I never sink to trickery. My motto is 'open covenants, openly arrived at'—if I may use a phrase he coined."

"Coined?" she snapped. "He picked that one out of Woodrow Wilson's pocket. But never mind. Just let's get this over with."

"Very well," Pietro said. "Desserts, then."

"Pies," she replied.

"Apple pies, perhaps?"

"No. Apple, mince, and pumpkin. And lemon meringue."

"I'll trade you the lemon meringue for two pumpkins," he offered, "plus a Duke Snyder and a Stan Musial."

"Throw in a Pete Rose and you've got a deal," Madeleine said, hooking out her pinkie. "But that's just because I'm being nice. Don't expect any more concessions."

"In that case," Pietro answered amiably, "we may as well proceed. Would you be so kind as to favor me with the Official List of Side Dishes?"

Madeleine took a deep breath. "Mashed potatoes, sweet potatoes…"

He interrupted her. "Will Madame have the sweet potatoes with or without the marshmallow and maraschino cherry *garniture*?"

Madeleine exhaled violently. "Will you cut that out?"

"Marmalade and whipped cream is also possible."

"I want plain buttered sweets. And I want you to just plain listen." She finished the list at top speed: "cubed turnips, creamed onions, red cabbage, Swiss chard, Brussels sprouts—and cranberry sauce."

Pietro did an elaborate double-take. "Cranberry sauce, Madame? Do I gather, then, that we will be serving sarsaparilla instead of wine?"

"Why?"

"Uncle Sturdy had a rule against drinking wine with jams and jellies."

"Uncle Sturdy can go fly his tombstone," Madeleine snorted. "I want wine *and* cranberry sauce. They both go perfectly well with turk—"

Pietro cut her off. "We agreed, I believe, to discuss the entrée only *after* the side dishes. Am I to assume that we have concluded this part of the negotiation?"

She hesitated. "Well...I guess so. But what if I think of something later on?"

"Now or never," Pietro said flatly. "No added starters."

"All right," she said. "That's that. Now for the entrée. I know you hate it, but this year we're having turkey."

"How about four ducks instead?" he suggested.

"You did that last year."

He ignored the comment. "A roast loin of pork, perhaps?"

"That was the year before."

"A country ham is always nice," he said, still trying.

"You fobbed that off on me three years ago, and I was thirsty for a week. And don't suggest goose or chicken, either. The entrée is turkey. Besides, it's patriotic. Benjamin Franklin in fact wanted to make it the National Bird."

"That only proves," Pietro said, "that even the brightest are not immune to dim ideas. If you really want to wave the flag, why don't we have roast eagle? It would certainly be different, and it could hardly taste worse."

"Thanksgiving is no time to be different," Madeleine huffed. "Anyway, you've flouted convention long enough. This time, you go along."

"Well then," he said, "I suppose that's it. We shall have the conventional turkey with the conventional stuffing and the conventional gravy—thus making the entire meal taste like food served at conventions."

"Oh, come on," she cajoled. "It's not all that bad."

Pietro thought for a moment. "I suppose you're right. There is one thing turkey has got to taste better than."

"What's that?" she asked.

Pietro leaned back and patted his stomach. "The crow, my love, that you have just managed to make me eat."

TWENTY ONE

THE KAISER ROLE

"You wouldn't happen to have another kaiser roll squirreled away somewhere, would you?" Pietro asked. "I think I need just one more sandwich to pep up the old system."

"In the bread drawer," Madeleine said, shaking her head disapprovingly. "But did it ever occur to you that your system might have more pep if you didn't clog it up with those ridiculous noontime eatouts? You're a writer, for crying out loud, not a body-builder."

Pietro was unfazed. "Recent studies have shown that pushing a pencil burns up as many calories as bench-pressing a stack of Bibles. And thinking burns up even more. I need fuel if I am to formulate a suitable answer to the question you just asked about abortion and capital punishment. Those are not, you must admit, light luncheon topics."

"Oh all right," Madeleine sighed. "Stoke up and get on with it."

Pietro assembled the sandwich silently, took a reflective bite, and set it down. "Delicious. Now as to the question. You ask why it so often happens that the very same people who vehemently oppose legislation to allow women a choice about terminating pregnancy are enthusiastic about laws that would allow the state to terminate the life of grownup criminals. The answer, I think, is anger."

"Anger?"

"Yes. Anger at the spectacle of people who, in their opinion, are getting away with murder. Or, to put it more broadly, a feeling of helpless rage at the presence of evil in the world—coupled with a false belief that both their helplessness and the world's evils could be removed if only the law would take a strap to the malefactors."

"What's so false about that? Are you going to say that the law shouldn't try to redress evil?"

"No, I'm not. Nor am I about to debate the morality of either abortion or capital punishment. If you like, for the purposes of this discussion, I shall concede not only that abortion is morally wrong, but also that executing murderers is scripturally defensible. My point, however, is that neither of those positions bears upon the answer to your question."

"Why not? If people believe what you just conceded, why shouldn't there be laws forbidding the one and allowing the other?"

Pietro frowned. "You are, I'm afraid, getting off the point in several directions at once. For one thing, not all members of present-day American society—not all, by a long shot—believe those things; therefore, it would be unwise for society to turn what is only the opinion of some into a rule that governs all. But that, too, is beside the point. Repeat your question, please, and you will see why."

Madeleine balked, then relented. "I asked, why do the same individuals..."

"Aha!" Pietro interrupted. "Do you see? Your question was not about the contradictory positions they take (forbidding medical murder of the unborn, but allowing judicial murder of the born); rather, it was about how one and the same individual could take those two positions and not be sensible of their contradiction."

"Okay, so I wandered a little. But then, you haven't exactly gotten a clarifying head of steam up yet, either. Maybe you should just eat and fuel up some more."

Pietro took another bite and suddenly held up the sandwich in triumph. "By George, you were right! Here's the answer right in front of us! People take those positions because they believe in the Kaiser Role."

"They believe in a bun?" Madeleine gasped, looking alarmed. "Stop eating this instant! The egg salad must be giving you brain poisoning."

"No, no," Pietro said soothingly. "Not r-o-l-l; r-o-l-e. As in, putting more trust in the role of Caesar than in the role of Christ."

"Maybe the ham was bad, too."

"Not at all. These individuals you ask about are

convinced that if only evil were sufficiently outlawed by the state, it would go away. And, since the state seems to them less than vigorous in its proscribing of evil, they become angry at its laxness. The state has failed them; accordingly, with all the wrath of little Caesars coming to set society straight, they try to force the state to become big Caesar with a vengeance."

"But don't they do all this in the name of Christ?"

"No. They do it in the name of a Christ conceived of as Caesar—thought of as a force-loving, score-evening, moral police-god who became incarnate to punch all the baddies in the nose and clean up the neighborhood. The real Christ, if you will cast your mind back, was somebody named Jesus who, besides claiming he came to save—not to judge the world—also ended up getting punched out himself—by the very law enforcement-types these people so eagerly expect to bring in the Kingdom."

"But isn't law essential to society?"

"Only up to a point. Human societies are fragile webs, held together more by the courtesies of civilization than by the armies of righteousness. Once those courtesies fall below a certain level, no amount of legal force can mend the damage to the web."

"What are you saying? That we may as well give up on the law because the web is already too badly broken?"

"Possibly. And, if it is, we shall find out soon enough. What I'm really saying, though, is that all the brouhaha raised by Christians in the name of enforcing the moral law is hazardous to the health of the Gospel. After this most recent presidential campaign, for example, I defy you to find more than three non-Christians in the country who would even suspect that the Gospel is about forgiveness rather than enforcement—or, for that matter, that it has any kind of good news at all."

"Isn't that a bit radical?"

"Who's to say? Sure, law should be based on morality. But, in the long run, the only thing strict morality is going to tell the world is that it's going to hell in a handbasket. I would have hoped that the Church—which has the antidote to that bad news in the free grace of a God who died for us while we were yet sinners—would not so easily have been tricked into hiding the light of its Gospel under a bushel of law."

"My, my," Madeleine said. "All that from a just a second sandwich! Tomorrow, remind me to limit you to one."

TWENTY TWO

THE RAW TRUTH

Pietro peeled two eggplants, sliced them up and began frying them in olive oil.

"You should never have married him," Madeleine's sister Gina said to her. "Someday he'll kill you with his short-cut cooking. He should be soaking those eggplants in salt water to get the poison out—the way Mamma always did, remember?"

"Contrary to your dire predictions," Pietro observed, "my cooking is totally safe. Not only has your sister remained hale and hearty since I married her; she's even a bit more substantial than when I sprung her from your mother's culinary superstition-trap."

Madeleine glowered at him. "If you say one more word about my weight, you're the one who won't be safe. And what do you mean, superstition-trap? Our mother was the best cook in North Queens."

"No offense," Pietro replied. "Your substantialities are

119

beautifully distributed, and I would also call your mother the finest cook in East, South and North Queens. It's just that she indulged in certain kitchen rituals that owed more to old wifery than to cookery."

"Like what?" Gina shot back.

"Well, for one thing, I seem to remember her cutting the end off a cucumber and rubbing it till it foamed—to get the toxins out, I believe."

"Oh, *that*," Gina conceded. "But eggplant is different. You can see the brown poison in the water you soak it in…"

"Of course," Pietro interrupted, "if you didn't soak it at all, and if you worked fast so the air didn't get at it, maybe there wouldn't be any brown color in the first place. And as for poison…"

Gina looked at him incredulously. "You mean, there isn't any?"

"Not a smitch."

"But then how did the superstition get started?"

Pietro turned his eggplant slices in the pan and added more olive oil. "The same way as all superstitions, my dear: The human race, being unable to handle the large evils that do exist, imagines for itself smaller, non-existent ones—and then invents rituals to make them go away. It produces a sense of power, I suppose: Mamma actually believes she's defending her wee ones from things that go bump in the eggplant."

"What's the harm, though?" Madeleine asked. "To me, it's just a nice little custom. Besides, I *like* to see the brown come out."

"No harm at all," Pietro answered, "unless you let it get between you and reality—in which case, it does a great deal of mischief indeed. It's one thing, for example, to step on cracks just for the fun of it; but if you seriously believe you're doing a number on your mother's back you have entered the dismal swamp of superstition."

Madeleine turned to Gina. "He may be right, you know. Mamma used to tell us that if we kept our galoshes on in the house, it would 'draw our eyes'. To this day, if I leave them on for two minutes, my eyeballs feel as if they're being dragged down to the floor."

"Yes," Gina volunteered. "And what about getting lockjaw if you cut the skin between your thumb and forefinger? I used to imagine it would take only one scratch and my bottom teeth would slam shut like a drawbridge. Still, though, culinary superstitions aren't *that* bad, are they?"

"Worse," Pietro said gravely. "In the other cases, experience eventually teaches you the truth. In cooking, however, the superstitions prevent the experience."

"He's getting theological, Gina," Madeleine said. "I'm afraid we've encouraged him."

"Truth is its own encouragement," Pietro declared. "Permit me to proceed. My maternal grandmother was English, as you know. Had you told her that her mind was practically destroyed by culinary myths, she would have laughed at you. But in fact, all the eggplantomancy in Sicily couldn't hold a candle to the ritual by which she sacrificed taste to safety."

"What *are* you talking about?" Gina exclaimed.

"The poor woman actually believed that *all* food was poison until it was cooked. Salads were unheard of in her home. And God help the child she caught eating raw potatoes or fresh lima beans. Even now, in ripeness and perfectness of age, I cannot shake the twinge of fear when I bite into an uncooked French fry."

"How did that ruin her cooking, though?" Gina asked.

"You were raised by an Italian mother and you can ask a question like that?" Pietro said. "Think of the things that you've eaten, but that her benighted soul couldn't bring itself even to try: pasta *al dente, pesto genovese,* pink lamb, rare beef, vegetables with crunch left in them—all because she devoutly believed that unless you boiled the hell out of everything, you'd go straight to your eternal punishment."

"Hey!" Madeleine said. "You lived with your grand-mother, didn't you? How come you managed to see the light?"

"I ate a half-cooked sprout once. It was so unlike Grandma's mushballs that the scales simply fell from my eyes: *Food was already safe! The goal of cooking was pleasure, not life insurance.*"

Pietro took a bite of raw eggplant.

Gina gasped.

Madeleine sighed.

TWENTY THREE

TV PREACHERS

Madeleine zapped the Sunday morning preacher with the remote. "Even though I can hardly stand that stuff," she said moodily, "I still have a funny feeling about it. Sometimes I wish Christianity could be as simple as they make it out."

Pietro had already started to leave the room. "The fact of the matter is," he said over his shoulder, "they don't make Christianity out to be simple at all. The Gospel is vastly, alarmingly, mind-numbingly simpler than the moralistic, judgment-loaded religion they're selling."

"So you say," she said, following him onto the porch. "But their stuff is at least selling, which is more than you can say for yours. Don't you ever wake up at three in the morning and wonder whether maybe—just maybe—they're doing something right?"

"Never," Pietro said decisively.

"But…"

Pietro cut her off. "I do not think such thoughts in the wee hours because, in my waking moments, I have canvassed the question and come up with a resounding 'No'."

"Fill me in then."

"Let me begin by making a distinction," Pietro said, settling himself for a smoke. "On the one hand, the broadcast evangelists are indeed doing something right, in both senses of the word. They are right—that is, *doctrinally correct,* as evangelists usually are—about rather a large number of important points: the Atonement accomplished by Jesus' death and resurrection, and so on. But they are also right, meaning *right of center,* on a great many theological and political questions."

"Stop playing with words and say something," Madeleine huffed.

"If you will allow me to finish my distinction..." Pietro cleared his throat for effect. "On the other hand, they are wrong to think that their rightness, of either kind, is worth much. Their incidental doctrinal correctness is vitiated by a profound missing of the main point of the Gospel, namely, salvation through *grace alone,* by *faith.* And their theologico-political rightism is miles away from true conservatism."

"Okay, so you're not playing. *Now* will you say something?"

"You must be patient with me, love. A cold brain, like a cold engine, needs a warm-up."

"*Floor it!*" Madeleine commanded; "or I'll floor *you!*"

Pietro suddenly became all business. "Let me take their political conservatism first. Conservatives conserve, of course. But true conservatives conserve major moral and political truths, not minor socio-cultural knick-knacks. As far as I'm concerned, what these electronic sermonizers are conserving is not the great principles on which America was founded—the Bill of Rights will do for a shorthand summary; rather, they're trying to conserve a bunch of Nineteenth Century social patterns. And in their zeal to recapture sentimentally-conceived, older mores, they are dangerously willing to give government, not to mention themselves, the right to knock heads, lock up questionable types, and generally make everybody's train—social, moral or esthetic—run according to their notion of what 'on time' means."

Madeleine shook her head. "I'm afraid they've got a lot of support out there."

"I *know* they've got a lot of support," Pietro said; "there has always been a well-traveled fascist right lane on the great American Way, and Big Brother can pick up all the hitchhikers he wants any day in the week. But Big Brother is no conservative. He's a bully; he works by threats and he rules by fear. Only *he*—he will tell you obligingly—only *his* program, only *his* devices can prevent disaster. Christ gave us his death and resurrection: He promised to save us *in* disaster, not out of it. For preachers to talk as if God will save America if only America will listen to their preaching, is to renege on their vocation. America—along with diplomacy and tact is not mentioned in the

Bible. You'd think they'd have noticed that."

"Not diplomacy or tact either, eh?" Madeleine quipped. "Lucky for you."

Pietro pressed on. "As I was saying. That brings me to the theological consideration. Of course the stuff they're peddling *sells*. *Religion* always sells. You can get people to buy almost any version of salvation-by-toeing-the-line you want to dream up. From 'Don't eat meat!' to 'Jog' to 'Pray six hours a day!' to 'Meditate' to 'Vote conservative' to 'No piggy things alone in the bathroom!' to 'Sacrifice a chicken on the solstice'—it will all go like hotcakes. Because the world *wants* to feel guilty, and the rulers of the darkness of this world are always happy to back up fresh batches of guilt to keep the troops in line."

"But…" Madeleine interjected.

"Nothing doing," Pietro snapped; "this is *my* 'but'." He took a deep breath. "*But*. The one thing you can never sell is *grace*. The human race would rather die than give houseroom to the outrage of *free acceptance, while we are yet sinners*. You can get people to buy acceptance *after their sins are under control*, or *only when their disasters have been forestalled by proper behavior*. But all the Gospel has to offer is acceptance *now*: *in* our sins and *in* our shipwrecks. And without condition. With no guilt left to be expiated and no good-deed lists asked for. You can always sell religion. But the Gospel of grace isn't religion and therefore you can't sell it for beans. Any gospel that *sells* is, by definition, *not* the Gospel."

"My, my," Madeleine said.

"Your, your, what? The whole sorry business is one of the oldest stories in Christianity. When St. Paul went out the back door of the church in Galatia, in the front door came a bunch of sales rep types from James and the Jerusalem church crowd. They had on polyester suits, they carried limp Bibles, and they were accompanied by three hundred Christian singers. And they said, 'We're so glad our brother Paul was able to spend some time with y'all. But he's a very busy man, and he's only able to give you the highlights of the faith. So we're here to fill you in on all the really important things without which you Gentiles are not going to make it to Salvation City. And so what did they give them? Circumcision. Kashruth. The Law. In a word, *religion*. And what did the Galatians do? They bought it like it was going out of style, which it already had—and which made them twice the fools Paul said they were."

Pietro ended triumphantly: "What do you think of *them* apples?"

"I think it's a good thing you're finished," Madeleine said threateningly. "If you'd gotten any more worked up, I would have had to zap you too."

TWENTY FOUR

TO FREEZE OR NOT TO FREEZE

The refrigerator was in its usual post-holiday state of glut: Pietro's gaze wandered over the thicket of half-filled peanut butter jars, wadded-up aluminum foil packages and nearly empty plastic bags with their tops in rank flower. Leftovers. A quarter of an acre of them, at least. He sighed diffidently and looked at Madeleine: "No chance I could serve you some of this for supper, I suppose?"

"Good supposing," she said, with not a trace of sympathy. "We've had that stuff for weeks. I want a new taste tonight. Make something from scratch. Chinese, I think. And stop keeping things around so long. All of those should have been frozen to begin with."

Pietro sighed again, this time so his mind wouldn't go from seethe to full boil. He was the working cook in this household; why couldn't he be the one to say what the larder should produce? Had the switching of roles in their marriage done nothing more than replace male chauvinism with female? He would start a movement.

NOMC. The National Organization of Male Cooks. Pants in the Pantry. The Female Diners Be Damned Club.

Actually though, it wasn't a sexist issue. Feminists might try to claim it for one, but anybody who cooked knew it was just a matter of the tyrant at the table versus the stiff at the stove. And it made no difference if the cook had a way with leftovers. His prowess (or hers) at raising dishes from the dead counted for nothing when Her (or His) Majesty ordered dinner.

And Pietro was good at it indeed. Nothing he served the second time was merely revived: it was resurrected. A stew came forth from the tomb renewed by fresh wine and spices; old pasta burst the bonds of death and appeared, Lazarus-like, as a golden *tortilla* with onions, cheese and eggs; a morbid roast of pork rose up sliced and glorified in a *sauce mole* graced with bitter chocolate and sherry. The only reason Her Royal Gourmandise balked at such miracles was that she knew what was in the refrigerator. The sight of the cold grave was too much for her. People like that should eat in restaurants where their weak faith isn't put to the test. They're not even told that Lazarus Lamb was dead; he is introduced as M. Emince d'Agneau and they're pleased to meet him. At $9.50 a throw à la carte, yet—for someone Pietro could get to make house calls for nothing.

Still, the Lady of his house did have a point. There was a measure of self-deception in his habit of squirreling away leftovers. It was not only Madeleine who decided she wanted some other cuisine than the pantry could provide. He himself sometimes looked at vintage lasagna and thought longingly of moo shee pork with Chinese doilies. But there was more to it than that. To tell the truth, he often cooked too much food on the pretext that he would do something with the surplus. When it came time, though—if, for example, he actually chose to resurrect the pasta—it somehow never looked like enough. So he compounded the felony by making too much all over again—producing thus, by a law of diminishing interest and increasing returns, leftover leftovers with no end in sight.

He remembered one particularly malignant growth of dish—a rice, then noodle, then cheese, then potato, then bread confection whose color went from white, to yellow, to an alarming orange and finally, a daunting brown—that Madeleine had released from the cycle of reincarnation by dumping over the porch railing. He took the hint and thenceforth restrained his tendency to overachieve. He even instituted periodic purges in which he not only got rid of dead dishes that might have been raised, but also did in some that were hardly wounded. So much he would grant in response to her criticism. But when it came to the subject of freezing leftovers instead of keeping them in the refrigerator, he dragged his feet.

To him, all that did was make them inaccessible to the creative cook.

Containers of chopped ham, cooked rice, leftover peas, and cold sauce supreme were, if they sat in the refrigerator, an invitation to artistry. They were stop-knobs on the Mighty Kitchen Wurlitzer; each ready, at a moment's inspiration, to contribute its music to the dish in composition. But rock-solid in the freezer, they were no more help than a jammed organ console. To have to bludgeon your way along just to get it even playable was a recipe only for exasperation.

He could see a point, of course, in freezing the remains of sauces: They were easy enough to melt; besides, they kept better that way. He also conceded the wisdom of freezing deliberately made leftovers sufficient to provide a meal at short notice. But beyond that, his freezer was for unprocessed food. As a cook, he considered himself a conductor, not a disc jockey. He brought his singers in from the cold and led them in new songs. Let somebody else settle for replaying not-so-golden oldies.

Maybe that was what lay at the bottom of his objection to the freezer as a repository of previous performances. It was a marvelous invention, but like all such technological advances, it tempted people not to unrealistic hopes for the future, but also to errors about the recapturability of the past. In extreme cases, it produced unadulterated silliness.

Every now and then, someone wrote an article about the possibility of freezing Einstein's brain—or even, if you could catch him after the right flight, the entire Kissinger. The idea was that in some future day, when the technology became available, we would be able to cope with the present by defrosting the personnel of the past. There was even a pseudo-scientific name for it: cryogenics.

Cryogeneticists would ward off Twenty-First Century menaces to national security by saying, "Watch out, or we'll thaw out Henry!" or, "Beware; we're putting the Ayatollah in the microwave!"

The trouble with that was that it confused resuscitation with resurrection. In the first place, this year's statesmen, kept on ice for decades, would not be useful, only out of date. Some of them were both right now, in fact. What was really called for in any present need—whether from the food freezer or the people fridge—was something better than the past, something risen and glorious that wasn't so likely to leave the same old dead taste in everybody's mouth.

Pietro decided to stick to his guns on not freezing leftovers. The past was never recapturable, so why encourage the attempt? Madeleine would just have to put up with his jars, bags and containers. No matter what she thought, they were his best, easiest shot at bringing new life out of old. How would she like it if, instead of trying to season their life afresh every day, he froze her for years against some need that might never arrive? That was a good question. He should ask her. For that matter, how would she like it if he froze himself?

That question, however, struck him as not so hot. He skipped it and went to work on the Chinese doilies.

TWENTY FIVE

TO DIE OR NOT TO DIE

Madeleine hung up the phone and put her head on the kitchen counter. "People!" she groaned as she pounded the surface with her fists.

Pietro was dicing celery with a Chinese cleaver. "I have a trusty blade here in my hand," he said. "Perhaps I could sally forth and avenge these wrongs you feel compelled to communicate to the Formica."

"Thanks a lot," Madeleine said, straightening up and going over to her chair. "But quite enough hatchet work has been done already. *That*, if you haven't already guessed, was Belinda."

"I gathered. What sewer gas was the original bad news bear trying to pump into the phone lines this time?"

"Well, it seems that she and Arthur are spearheading a congregational movement to get rid of their minister."

"Aha!" Pietro exclaimed. "What has the poor Domine done? Preached heresy? Dipped his hand into the church till? Appeared drunk and disorderly in public?"

"He's getting divorced and remarried—to the church treasurer's present wife."

"And Belinda, I presume, finds the reverend gentleman's plans for his own life a bit too rich for her blood—despite the fact that, as I recall, her very own Arthur was divorced when she married him."

"It's all hypocrisy," Madeleine snorted. "The old double standard. The clergy get crucified for doing what the laity find perfectly okay for themselves."

"Except," Pietro interrupted, "that I am sure Belinda doesn't see it that way. I'll bet you this pile of diced celery that she thinks Arthur's divorce and remarriage was brave, clean and reverent, while the minister's was nasty, brutish and far too short on lead time."

"Exactly," Madeleine said. "And scandalous to boot. He and the treasurer's wife have been seen together in The Shady Nook."

Pietro put on his best shocked-beyond-words look. "Oh, well. In that case I have to agree with Belinda. The things that restaurant tries to palm off as food! This clergyman obviously has no taste at all."

"Will you please be serious?" Madeleine implored. "What would *you* have said to her?"

"Well," Pietro answered, "I would have tried to explain to her that the largest scandal involved is not the minister's but hers. He is, at worst, just one more sinner to whom the church is sent to proclaim Jesus' forgiveness. She, however, is in a fair way to becoming convinced that the church is sent only to the righteous."

"All she'd say to that," Madeleine observed, "would be that his sin is somehow beyond the pale."

Pietro smiled. "Then I would inquire where she got that distinction. All church services, to the best of my knowledge, contain a confession of sin in which the congregation, with one heart, mind, and mouth, proclaim that, collectively and individually, they all stink on ice. None of those confessions, however, singles out certain sins as worse than others."

"You wouldn't try to convince her that maybe the minister's divorce and remarriage isn't sinful? After all, she probably doesn't know beans about what's really involved."

"That is quite correct," Pietro said. "But to say so to Belinda is simply to fall into the trap she's dug for herself. It's just capitulating to her you-can't-be-saved-unless-you-can-prove-you're-a-good-guy argument. Her minister was a sinner before this situation, and he will no doubt be one after it. The church has to be told loud and clear that tossing out sinners is a violation of the Gospel of grace. Not to mention the fact that it's stupid: A church that can't manage to stay in communion with sinners makes about as much sense as a carpenter who can't stand to handle wood."

"I know what she'd say to that, though. She'd say that the minister and the treasurer's wife should at least have had the decency to lie low and wait a while—to show their repentance, I suppose, and to give everybody a chance to forgive and forget."

Pietro shook his head. "No go. If God doesn't wait to forgive, neither should the church. The Prodigal made his confession *after* his father fell on his neck and kissed him. The Publican is justified *on the spot,* just for saying he's no good; he isn't told to stay away from the temple until he can come back with the Pharisee's speech in his pocket. Jesus tells us to pray that we will be forgiven *as we forgive:* If we insist on withholding forgiveness until we can manage to forget other people's sins, then in effect we're asking God to hold off forgiving us until his omniscience gets feeble-minded enough not to remember our own sins. By some estimates, that could be a long time."

"But doesn't God say he'll forget our sins and remember our iniquities no more?"

"Precisely," Pietro said. "And in Jesus on the cross he does indeed forget: He drops dead to our sinfulness— major, minor, or in between. I would suggest to Belinda that she might do well to follow his example vis-à-vis her minister."

"What? Drop dead?"

"That would do the trick nicely," Pietro replied. "But so would just shutting up on the whole subject—which option I would offer her as a less drastic alternative."

"It's sad though, isn't it?" Madeleine mused. "I mean, why do they always single out clergy with public sins and kill them?"

"Sad is not exactly the right word. The name of the Gospel game is death and resurrection. Anyone who accepts death gets resurrection. If Belinda's minister has a grip on the Gospel, he'll be one hundred percent safe in Jesus, even if he ends up selling shoes from a matchbook cover ad. He will say to his congregation exactly what Jesus might have said to Caiaphas: 'I have to thank you; even though you've handed me a personal inconvenience, it's going to be a major career advancement.'"

Madeleine frowned. "That sounds like a recommendation to crucify people in the name of the Gospel."

"No, it's a recommendation to Belinda to work on her own dying and stop cheering for other people's. At present, she is a member of the First Church of Caiaphas, Inc. Who knows? If she ever decides to get out of that bad news outfit, she might actually rise up and be able to breathe fresh air instead of sewer gas."

TWENTY SIX

THE 92ND STREET ENFORCER

"Where is it written," Madeleine asked testily, "that nobody is allowed to even think of improvements on your mother's Christmas cookie recipes? All I suggested was dipping the butter jobbies in a little melted chocolate."

Pietro looked up from the tattered, loose-leaf binder. "It is written in the history of my family," he said. "We do not stoop to putting decorations on our Christmas cookies."

"Why?" she objected. "Decorations are some kind of sign of the collapse of taste?"

"Precisely, my love. And my family were among the last fighters against them. It was a losing battle, of course, but the best years of my childhood were spent on the ramparts of a veritable bastion of Christmas cookie purity."

"What on earth are you talking about?"

"My boyhood in Queens on 92nd Street, between Roosevelt Avenue and Polk, as it then was—before somebody degraded it to 37th Avenue. Ah, what a block that was for cookies!"

"What was so terrific about them?"

"Their unadorned purity, that's what," Pietro said as his eye took on a gleam. "We kept the faith, even though we were surrounded by lesser breeds without the law. The people on 93rd Street actually made cookies with colored sugar all over them. Our mothers used to warn us: 'Eat the cookies outside; if you go into their houses, the floral wallpaper will get you'. We were raised by people who cared, you see."

"You were raised by a bunch of snobs, as far as I'm concerned."

"You can say that," Pietro went on solemnly, "only because you were not there to see the danger to manners, morals, and sound doctrine. 93rd Street was bad enough, but beyond that...well, if I told you what they put on their Christmas cookies on 94th Street, then you'd understand."

"So tell me," she yawned.

"This is no yawning matter, Maddie. Our parents were all vigilance, let me tell you. I remember well the night they sent me to bed without my supper on account of a Santa cookie I unsuspectingly accepted from Mary Jane Rafferty. They were about to let me off with just a warning about playing with the strange children of those 'strange people on 94th Street', but I made the mistake of producing the cookie and saying that I thought the chocolate sprinkle and silver shot were pretty."

Pietro paused.

"And…?" she asked.

"The scene is almost too painful to recount."

"Be brave. You'll probably get through it."

"Well," he said, "my mother fainted dead away on the spot, and I was ordered straight to my room. It was only hours later, after my father had steadied her with repeated dosages of Remy Martin, that he came up and spoke with me."

Pietro hesitated again.

"Don't give out now," she said encouragingly. "You're almost there. What did he say?"

Pietro squared his shoulders. "He said to me, 'Son, you're young, I know. But believe me, if you don't get this bathos out of your system before you're five, it'll be the end of us all. Chocolate sprinkles on Christmas cookies are a crime, my boy. And silver shot just compounds the felony. Forget this 94th Street wanderlust of yours. Forget Mary Jane Rafferty. And by all that's holy, never, never go near 95th Street'."

"What'd they have there," Madeleine asked, "sea monsters and anthropophagi?"

"Worse," Pietro said, lowering his voice. "I went to 95th Street once. It was the last time I ever disobeyed my parents. The whole block was populated by madmen and people from other planets. You could smell tripe cooking at eleven in the morning, and the kids there told you horror stories about eating beef hearts stuffed with prunes."

"The cookies," Madeleine reminded him. "What

about the cookies?"

"Ah, they were the worst thing of all," he said with a shudder. "Gingerbread Christmas trees with blue icing and tiny marshmallow snowballs all over them. I ran straight home without stopping and cried myself to sleep. But then in the morning…"

"Don't tell me there's more?"

"Yes indeed. In the morning, I rose convinced of my calling to defend my native block against the evil of decoration. I went across the street to my Aunt Lotte's for cookies and milk, and she was making spice drops. When she got out the confectioner's sugar to roll them in, I said to her, 'Aunt Lotte, don't you think that makes them look sort of, well…96th Street?' I tell you, you never saw powdered sugar go back in the pantry so fast in your life."

"You were just a charming little kid, weren't you?"

"Charming, yes; but more important, truth-loving. My next step," Pietro continued, "was Mrs. Franzini's, three houses up. I had to be firm with her. She was sprinkling white nonpareils on some molasses cookies, and when I gasped, she got all nervous. 'Look, Petey,' she said, 'make believe you didn't see them. At least they're not mixed colors.' So I very calmly said to her, 'Nonpareils are nonpareils, Mrs. Franzini. If you want to spend another Christmas here on 92nd Street, you better straighten up. Of course, if you take them off right now and give me some Hershey's for my milk, I could forget to tell my mother."

"You must've been as popular as tooth decay,"

Madeleine said. "Is there supposed to be a moral to this story?"

"Yeah," Pietro said in a hoarse, gravely voice. "The moral is, you should think a lot more about Mrs. Franzini and a lot less about slopping chocolate on my butter cookies. Otherwise, I might make you an offer you can't refuse on 97th Street."

TWENTY SEVEN

PUDDING: THE FUTURE IN PERSPECTIVE

Madeleine, Pietro thought, would be delighted. She loved plum puddings.

He put the candied orange peel down next to the cutting board and surveyed the ingredients for his plum puddings. The *mise en place,* as the French called it, was an insider's delight: Only the cook got to see, touch, and taste the emphatic uniqueness that went into a dish. He munched a raisin.

Good, he thought; except for the price. Raisins had followed gold and oil right up through the roof. No sense complaining, though. It might cost him eight times what it did his grandmother to turn out Christmas puddings, but it was still a bargain. He'd managed to pick up ten small bowls for $1.50 a piece: Those, filled with $20.00 worth of ingredients, would make this year's gifts to the assorted apples of his eye.

At $3.50 a head, plus labor and love, they were the

perfect present for people who knew money wasn't everything.

He did a quick check through his grandmother's recipe before starting: One pound each of kidney suet, bread crumbs, sugar (brown and white, mixed), Muscat raisins, seedless raisins, currants and candied peel (orange, lemon and citron); six apples, chopped, eight eggs, a cup of flour, a wineglass of cognac, and salt, cinnamon and clove to taste. He had more than enough of almost everything; just to be on the safe side of ten finished puddings, he decided to throw in a pound of dried apricots and go heavy on the other ingredients wherever it made sense. These old recipes encouraged that sort of thing: You put back the cup you ordinarily measured flour with and got out a monster coffee mug; a ten-ounce burgundy glass replaced the six-ounce white wine for cognac; and the spices got pinched with three fingers instead of two. With a little finagling you could end up with half again as much and still claim you'd followed the recipe to the letter.

He got out the knife and went to work, first on the suet, then on everything else that needed chopping. These mid-December Christmas preparations, it occurred to him, were the best part of the holidays. The days were full; presents accumulated in drifts all over the house; and each week brought forth new smells and tastes: puddings early on; then cookies, batch by batch; and finally the yeast breads that proclaimed the feast at the door.

By contrast, though, the feast itself often turned out to be a downer. He thought back to Thanksgiving. For him, the greatest pleasures had been the days of planning beforehand, and the hours spent cooking. The meal itself came a slow second, even though it was good. And the time after dinner had been purely and simply a drag. People watched TV or fell asleep. It wasn't just after sex that every animal was sad: After a festal dinner, glumness congealed over everybody like cold gravy.

He wondered why. The usual answer blamed it on the exceptional quantities of food and drink, but that couldn't be the reason. It was possible to ingest far more food than at a holiday dinner and still be bright-eyed and bushy-tailed. On one memorable evening, he and some friends had consumed two large pizzas a piece, plus enough beer to drown the Matterhorn, and the party got nothing but jollier all night long.

Perhaps, he thought, it was the impromptu nature of that evening that made it different. Nobody had spent weeks building up expectations for it. But that wasn't quite the answer either. People did indeed anticipate feast days; but if they were honest they would admit they seldom expected too much from the feast itself.

Rather early in life, most of us came to the conclusion that the less we looked forward to enjoying holiday afternoons, the better off we would be. They were just like Sundays, only worse: no funnies.

Still though, if people didn't have excessive expectations for a holiday, why did they go right on suffering from post-festal tristesse? Why was it they could prepare for it happily enough for weeks or months, only to fold up when it finally came? He had read somewhere that the incidence of deaths actually rose after holidays. Not just from suicide, but from so-called natural causes as well. The future, apparently, kept us going only as long as it didn't arrive. Once it got here, it was a killer.

He finished chopping the ingredients and started mixing everything together in a twelve-quart pot. For someone who claimed to delight in festal preparations, he was thinking dark thoughts indeed. Nevertheless he would try to work it out in his mind. What was the trick? Was it to stay away from feasts altogether? Was there some way to keep the future from arriving? Or was it perhaps to pick up the idea of the future in a different way?

That was more like it. The mistake we made about the future was to think of it as a time to come—as a kind of good ship lollipop that would, on a certain day, sail up and unload its cargo. That kept us happy enough through the days of waiting, but on the day itself it left us with a problem. And not just because the goodies might fail to be delivered. Rather because, even if they were, the very act of delivery left us sitting in a present with no more future to look forward to. A cargo cult that actually worked was even worse than one that didn't: It was a self-defeating prophecy.

The future therefore—at least the future as an engine of our happiness—was not a time to come; it was a hope in the present. The essence of it was not that it would or would not happen some day, but that we believed in it resolutely enough to let it keep us going now. The trouble then, with parking the future at some particular time was that when the date finally arrived, it turned out to be the one kind of day nobody needed: a futureless present that by necessity brought hope—and with it life—to a grinding halt.

In other words, as long as we located the future in the present, we were safe. It was future futures that made the mischief. He thought of the early Christians and their hope for the second coming of Christ. People wondered why, when Jesus failed to show up, they didn't get depressed. The answer was that they had never thought of his return as a future event; rather, it was a present fact in their lives. It was as if they were at a party and their host had said, "Excuse me; I'm going out to the kitchen to get a can of smoked oysters and a bottle of Scotch. I'll be back in a minute." They kept right on partying—enjoying their present—because they didn't make the mistake of trying to figure out which minute he meant. Instead they said, "He's coming back! Isn't that terrific?"

Therefore, the trick of getting through feast days without sadness was to refuse to let them become futureless presents. What that meant in practice was that you allowed them to suffuse all the days before the feast with brightness, purpose, cinnamon and clove; but then you were careful to remember that the feast day itself needed a future too. Holidays were not ends in themselves, not points at which we stop. Rather, they were training devices to break us of the habit of stopping. That was, no doubt, why the greatest feasts had the longest preparation: Advent before Christmas and Lent before Easter. Getting there was half the fun. And not kidding yourself that you'd arrived was the rest of the lesson. Maybe that was why plum puddings were flamed with Cognac: They were lights that invited us, at the darkening end of the feast, to hope for the future again.

He packed the bowls with pudding mixture, tied on covers made from an old bedsheet and set them to steam for six hours in an assortment of pots and pans.

Time to sit back and have a glass of…he caught himself. If there was any truth in all this, that was exactly what it was not time for. Too many arrivals of that sort and there'd be no motion at all. Suffuse the present with the future instead: Madeleine looked forward to the sweet, cognac-laced Hollandaise sauce he served with the puddings even more than plum pudding itself. Why not write out a copy of his grandmother's recipe to go with each one as an extra gift? He fetched his mother's hand-written cookbook from the shelf and copied it out in all its brevity:

> 4 egg yolks, 2 Tbs. cream, 2 Tbs. Cognac, 4 Tbs. sugar, pinch of salt.
> Place in a pot and whisk well—off the fire. Then whisk well, on and off the fire, until the custard stage is reached.
> Back away, whisking as you go, and add 8 Tbs. butter. Beat until blended in. Serve.

There. With all that backing and whisking, it would be a present to keep them moving into the future, even after Christmas dinner. Madeleine would be doubly pleased.

ACKNOWLEDGEMENTS

For the publication of this book, we are indebted first and foremost to Robert's wife, Valerie Capon, who so generously chose us to help resurrect his work. Thank you to the Rev. Mark Strobel who helped spark this project and served faithfully as the middleman for our correspondences. Thank you to the Rt. Rev. C. Andrew Doyle and the Episcopal Diocese of Texas, for their support of Mockingbird and especially of this project; to David Peterson and Margaret Pope for copyediting; to CJ Green for the layout and formatting; to all of our readers, donors, and supporters—thank you.

ABOUT MOCKINGBIRD

Founded in 2007, Mockingbird is an organization devoted to connecting the Christian faith with the realities of everyday life in fresh and down-to-earth ways. We do this primarily, but not exclusively, through our publications, conferences, and online resources. To find out more, visit us at mbird.com or e-mail us at info@mbird.com.

ALSO FROM MOCKINGBIRD

The Mockingbird Quarterly
edited by Ethan Richardson

Churchy: The Real Life Adventures of a Wife, Mom, and Priest
by Sarah Condon

Mockingbird at the Movies
edited by C.J. Green and David Peterson

Law and Gospel: A Theology for Sinners (and Saints)
by Will McDavid, Ethan Richardson, and David Zahl

A Mess of Help:
From the Crucified Soul of Rock N'Roll
by David Zahl

Eden and Afterward: A Mockingbird Guide to Genesis
by Will McDavid

PZ's Panopticon:
An Off-the-Wall Guide to World Religion
by Paul F.M. Zahl

The Mockingbird Devotional:
Good News for Today (and Everyday)
edited by Ethan Richardson and Sean Norris

Grace in Addiction:
The Good News of Alcoholics Anonymous for Everybody
by John Z.

This American Gospel:
Public Radio Parables and the Grace of God
by Ethan Richardson

*Our books are available at www.mbird.com/publications or on Amazon, and
our quarterly magazine can be found at magazine.mbird.com.*